Praise for

The Shape of my Eyes

"Dave's story pulls you in because it's all our story—finding identity and home. . . . Dave does the best kind of deconstruction—not one of religion or God but of himself."

—Bob Roberts Jr., president, GlocalNet / Multi-Faith
Neighbors Network / Glocal Ventures /
Institute for Global Engagement

"I devoured the book in just a few days, captivated by the raw vulnerability Dave courageously shares with his readers. It's astounding to see how he opens up about his deepest pains and wounds, making us wonder about the immense courage it must have taken to lay bare such personal struggles. . . . It is certain to touch millions of lives and families, just as it has profoundly impacted ours."

—Patrick and Joyce, Bangkok, Thailand, Amway Crown
Ambassadors and serial entrepreneurs in
education, wellness, and sustainable

"*The Shape of My Eyes* is a compelling and introspective memoir that gracefully navigates the complexities of identity, cultural heritage, and the journey of self-discovery. . . . A powerful and uplifting must read for anyone committed to the hard, hopeful work of building a better world."   —Sylvia Kim, founder and CEO, Rebel For Good

"Dave's vulnerability and candidness adds to the spiritual authority he carries, and I'm sure the Holy Spirit will speak to you as you dive into his spiritual story. Prepare to be challenged, inspired, and have your outlook expanded."

—Teofilo Hayashi, founder of Dunamis Movement, senior leader of Zion Church

"*The Shape of My Eyes* relays Dave Gibbons's intimate origin story of growing up in a multicultural America that struggled and continues to struggle to accept him and those of third cultures. Struggling with Identity and the labels others have placed on him, David encourages us on our journey, sometimes in spite of the challenges and heaviness of American Christian culture. David navigates the complex issues of Faith, identity, and following a path in spite family adversity and pain."

—Lawrence Ho

"This is a book about pain, suffering, reflection, perseverance, and resilience.... Through his openness and willingness to be vulnerable, Dave creates a narrative that is as relatable as it is inspiring and makes the reader feel intimately connected to his experiences. This book is for anyone grappling with questions of personal identity or searching for their purpose amidst confusion. Highly recommended for its heartfelt honesty and transformative insight."

—Matthew Shampine, cofounder and CEO of DNK

"An iconic narrative of a Korean American growing up in America—incredibly honest and vulnerable.... You will not be able to put it down"   —Paul Kim, investor and founder

"As much of America, and the American church, struggles with issues of race, immigration, pluralism, and spirituality, we need to hear stories like Dave Gibbons's. With disarming honesty, deep self-reflection, and hard-won wisdom, Gibbons reveals the blessings and burdens of growing up in a mixed-race family while navigating the racist subculture of Christian fundamentalism to find a more authentic life with God. With this memoir, Dave Gibbons reveals why he's uniquely gifted to be a leader of leaders."

—Skye Jethani, award-winning author, cohost of *The Holy Post* podcast, and cofounder of Holy Post Media

"Dave Gibbons's memoir goes beyond the scope of most stories, documenting the role that suffering played in his development and his journey to peace and healing through grace and forgiveness. Gibbons's use of tender prose and sincere storytelling allows him to explore how racism, familial trauma, and rejection cause pain that has the potential to affect individuals for years to come. Ultimately, *The Shape of My Eyes* is a story of hope, showing how God's patient compassion led Gibbons to a place of peace and wholeness through reconciliation. Infused with vulnerability and light-heartedness, this memoir has the potential to unleash healing in readers of all backgrounds."

—Dave Ferguson, founder of Exponential conference and author of *B.L.E.S.S.: 5 Everyday Ways to Love Your Neighbor and Change the World*

"Because there are no road maps for life, we seek the opinions of our family, friends, teachers, mentors, and prominent individuals. Dave Gibbons is a servant-leader living in our midst, helping us to orient, navigate, and materialize our ways of life. Most importantly, he is accessible to all of us regardless of our respective differences."

—June Elizabeth Kang, TV personality, host of *June Kang's Good Life*, author of 내가말해줄게, wife to actor Choi Min Soo, mother of two sons

"Dave Gibbons possesses a once-in-a-generation depth of intellect and soul. Through his vivid storytelling, specificity morphs into moments of universal connection. Dave—in his leadership, speaking, and writing—always finds a way to make people feel seen and beloved, just as they are."   —Melody Hahm, Harlem Capital

"Raw and poignant, this memoir hits palpably close to home. Dave proves once again that vulnerability is powerful and our brokenness is the singular thread that knits us all together."

—Jason Y. Lee, founder, CEO, Jubilee Media

The Shape of my Eyes

The Shape of my Eyes

A Memoir of Race, Faith, and Finding Myself

Dave Gibbons

WORTHY
PUBLISHING

New York • Nashville

Worthy
Hachette Book Group
1290 Avenue of the Americas, New York, NY 10104
worthypublishing.com
twitter.com/worthypub

First edition: July 2024

Worthy is a division of Hachette Book Group, Inc. The Worthy name and logo are registered trademarks of Hachette Book Group, Inc.

The publisher is not responsible for websites (or their content) that are not owned by the publisher.

Worthy Books may be purchased in bulk for business, educational, or promotional use. For information, please contact your local bookseller or the Hachette Book Group Special Markets Department at special.markets@hbgusa.com.

The poem "Night" by Kevin Schaal has been reprinted with permission of the author.

Scripture taken from the New King James Version®. Copyright © 1982 by Thomas Nelson. Used by permission. All rights reserved.

Print book interior design by Bart Dawson

Library of Congress Cataloging-in-Publication Data

Names: Gibbons, Dave, 1962– author.
Title: The shape of my eyes : a memoir of race, faith, and finding myself / Dave Gibbons.
Description: First edition. | New York : Worthy, 2024.
Identifiers: LCCN 2023051887 | ISBN 9781546003236 (hardcover) |
    ISBN 9781546003250 (ebook)
Subjects: LCSH: Gibbons, Dave, 1962– | Clergy—United States—Biography. |
    Korean Americans—Biography. | Christian biography—United States.
Classification: LCC BR1725.G437 A3 2024 | DDC 280 [B]—dc23/eng/20240126
LC record available at https://lccn.loc.gov/2023051887

ISBNs: 9781546003236 (hardcover), 9781546003250 (ebook)

Printed in Canada

MRQ

Printing 1, 2024

Dedicated to those searching for home

Contents

Contents

Prologue

An uneasiness rose inside me. My heart started racing and a cold sheen of sweat traced its way down my forehead. The very air seemed laden with a sense of dread.

I didn't want to go anywhere, and I didn't want to see anyone. In a mere hour, people would be showing up to hear me speak at our church's twentieth-anniversary celebration. The pressure to deliver a spectacular talk, mixed with disappointment about not having our own property at this stage of our existence, stirred an emptiness in me.

Maybe I'd feel better once I got to church. I tried to convince myself that I'd had this feeling before, and it had been okay. I considered trying to make myself go, but it really felt different this time. I just I couldn't do it. I called one of the staff, my voice shaky.

"Abe, I don't think I can come today. I'm not feeling well."

I couldn't tell him how I was really feeling. I considered what people would think of me if I didn't show up and how I would explain this dark place that I found myself in.

I can't reveal all my anxiety.

I was used to being the strong one.

Abe was caught off guard, but assured me that he'd take care of things.

"You okay, Dave?" he asked.

"Yes, I think so. Thanks, Abe." I didn't want to say anything more. All I knew was that I wasn't well.

I'd never missed an event like this before. I was dependable. I consistently met deadlines and expectations. My personal credo was that just showing up is a large part of "crushing it" in the world. Abe had never heard me sound like this in the twenty years we had known each other, and I'm sure he was baffled as to why I needed the rest of the morning to try and pull myself together.

I didn't understand it, either.

As I lay in the sanctuary of my bed, trying to make sense of what was happening, I realized that the anniversary celebration for our church was clearly unearthing feelings and expectations I had buried. Our church is not a normal church. We are culturally diverse and young. We pride ourselves on being a church for those who don't usually like church. And even though outwardly it appeared that our unique community was successful, I was constantly struggling not having our own facility or property to call our own. We had moved locations dozens of times. We could boast that we were a Southern California megachurch, but in reality, our real impact in the city or in the world seemed minuscule. I had been told I would need to raise an enormous amount of money for the facility of our dreams. These were the immediate, more tangible things I could point to catalyzing these intense feelings of panic.

Panic.

There it was.

Was I having a panic attack? I pulled out my laptop to google my symptoms. Disorientation. Nausea. Sweating. I was having a panic attack. I realized this had happened to me before, but I had never recognized it as a full-fledged panic attack. I thought it was some type of normal nervousness or the kind of fear that envelopes everyone occasionally. Just a case of heightened anxiety.

I knew it was going to take some time for me to unravel this moment of revelation. I knew that moment that there were deeper things about my past that were unresolved.

My life had always been oriented toward the future. That's how I was taught as a child. Things like the Rapture, Jesus' second coming, heaven, and the afterlife are a part of my daily cycle of meditations. When I started consulting and launching some companies, I was future oriented as well. Entrepreneurs are rewarded and celebrated for being visionary, for being ahead of others in predicting future trends and movements. So naturally this became my life orientation, my identity: the visionary and futurist leader.

What I was experiencing this morning had little to do with the future. It dealt with my past. My parents. My religion. The clashing of cultures. The dichotomy of East and West. Race and heritage. Unexpected pain. And my eyes. The myriad of people, events, and cultural experiences chosen for me were not of my volition.

There was something else. Since I'd become a spiritual guide, my ears had been opened to the anguish of countless tragedies and traumas. These stories and whispered secrets had taken residence in my soul. They had done something to me. Their effect was hard to perceive at the time because I was entirely focused on listening and understanding others' pain. I was not yet cognizant of what hearing those stories was doing to me.

I was experiencing a very real phenomenon called vicarious trauma, where experts say you can take a significant percentage of the trauma of others into your own body. When someone shared their pain with me, it would stay with me for days, even weeks. Back when I started pastoral work, I would line up my counseling all in one day.

I soon learned that I would be wrecked for days after these sessions. Digesting the suffering and trauma took a toll on me every time I listened to someone who was hurting.

What do you do with a wife's pain as she talks about her husband's sexual abuse of their daughter as he quietly sits next to her, looking down at the floor with shame?

What do you do with all the anger and worry when you're called to intervene in a marital dispute? The wife answering the door, still breathing heavily from an intense argument, sweating and crying, with a deep gash across her forehead. The wound is still fresh, white, and starting to bleed. How does someone make sense of that?

Where do you place the anguish from the pain of seeing a young couple in the emergency room holding their lifeless daughter in their arms?

How do you cope with the shocked teenage children telling you that their father just murdered their mother?

Vicarious trauma is real.

Even on that Sunday morning, I understood there was unfinished work processing my past that had unearthed this panic attack.

I knew there was more to it than my experiences as a pastor. I already understood on some level that the root cause had to do with my own family. With my Korean mom and Midwestern American father, and the merging of their cultures that is in my DNA. The fusion of their stories, their marriage, their suffering, and their secrets is embedded in me.

I'm Dave Gibbons. A Korean American. I look 100 percent Korean. Yet my father is white and my mom Asian. I'm married with four beautiful children. I've traveled to many places in America and spent a lot of time in Asia and South America. I love to eat bibim-naengmyeon, cold noodles mixed in a spicy gochujang-based sauce mixed with vegetables, yet love my hamburgers, too. It's fun exploring cultures, but home to me can be anywhere my family and friends are. I think laughter is healing and holy. I do work that makes me look like an extrovert, but I'm an introvert who loves being by himself for long periods of time. I work in multiple worlds, from the religious realm to the arenas of business, professional sports, and entertainment. I'm unusual to some people because I'm a pastor and I also lead a business where I consult, write, and speak. I love working with creative and thoughtful people in diverse cultures and spheres. My advisement work has been with venture capital companies, hedge fund managers, professional athletes, and entertainers. That's my work. But over time, all this work with people simply exposed things in my personal life that needed deeper examination. This book examines the awkward and hazardous dance of finding myself in the midst of cultures, family, and religion. Yes, religion. The topic of conversation often hard to discuss without a fight. My hope is that sharing my journey into the roots of evangelical, American Christianity will shed light and understanding into a culture that has become a political and economic juggernaut. My intent is not to belittle the culture or anyone associated with it. I became a part of it and was certainly caught up in the zeitgeist of it all.

To be candid, writing this book was an opportunity to reexamine my beliefs and perspectives. Narratives of old stories I told had new meaning when I took the time to sit in a scene and thoughtfully consider the sounds, the characters involved, and the details of how each person would respond in that specific situation. Since this is a memoir, this is my perspective. This book has gone through multiple versions and countless pep talks. I took the liberty to change some names and several events slightly to safeguard the privacy of those who inhabit these pages and to fill in the gaps of my memories. I hope that in my story you might find a piece of your own story.

So here we go. My earliest story begins in Seoul, South Korea.

CHAPTER ONE

Between Two Worlds

In Korean culture, a child's first birthday is marked with exuberant celebration. In the past many children did not survive their first year. If they did, their first birthday—called dol (돌잔치)—was celebrated with a party to commemorate that the child had made it despite the harsh conditions of the war-torn country. I was born into this divided nation on February 28, 1962, when families were torn apart due to the Korean War: Parents from children. Brothers from sisters. Husbands from wives. The thirty-eighth parallel divides the North and the South, and still remains this way today.

The Armistice between North Korea and South Korea was signed nine years before my birth. I was designated as a mixed-race baby—the type of baby who might have been thrown into a trash can or left at the door of an orphanage just a few years earlier. US soldiers would have relations with the Korean women, and unwanted children became part of the fruit of postwar Korea. The shame and social stigma associated with these children would be unbearable, and women abandoned their babies in great numbers.

Fortunately, I was part of the next generation of postwar children. My father, an Air Force man, arrived in Seoul soon after the Korean War. I had an American father who wanted me and a Korean mom who was treated lovingly by her American husband. When I was born in Seoul, I became the embodiment of East and West to my mom and dad. The best of both worlds. A symbol of hope to my father, who didn't have a dad, and my mom, who like my dad, grew up in poverty. I became part of a rising tide of misfits coming out of the Korean War who had parents of both Asian and American descent.

A Korean child's first birthday is celebrated with an array of traditional Korean meats and side dishes, stacks of fruit, and dduk—special rice cakes. The baby is dressed in the finest hanbok—traditional Korean clothes made of colorful silks and linens. Guests bring gifts of money and rings made of pure gold. The highlight of the party is not the baby smashing the birthday cake but the first birthday baby grab known as doljabi (돌잡이). A tray of specially selected items is carefully positioned in front of the baby, and everyone waits in anticipation until the baby crawls and chooses one. Whichever item the child grabs is said to symbolize the baby's future career or fate. Each item has a different meaning. Some represent jobs, and some represent skills or a particular lifestyle. There's a traditional set of items, but these days it seems anything goes, as people add toy golf clubs to represent a golf teacher or a pro golfer or add a computer mouse to symbolize a programmer or maybe a professional video game player or a paintbrush for the future artist. The degree of how seriously each family considers the baby's choice varies from family to family, but the selection of items and their meanings are special to each family.

The items used by most households back in my day were money, signifying that the child would be wealthy; food, meaning they would not go hungry; a pencil, meaning they would become a scholar; and thread, which was believed to symbolize that they would live a long life. On my first birthday, I was all about the money.

My parents said that photographing me on this momentous occasion was hilariously difficult. My round head, a third of the size of my whole body, kept tilting to one side, with the rest of my body following. I resembled a Jell-O figure, wiggly and floppy. I would be positioned upright ever so gently on a crisp, white bedsheet, erect for a few seconds, then promptly fall over, oblivious of the photographic requirements. My proud Korean mother laughed so hard, she cried.

대브 Daebu was what they called me. It's an affectionate Korean way of pronouncing my name, David. Many Korean American boys in my generation were called David or John or Sam. Boys in Korea are treasured and desired; women are given a higher status if they have a son instead of a daughter. They had thought I was going to be a girl, so they had a set of girl clothing ready and planned to call me Karen. My parents gave me, and eventually my brother, Doug, a common American name so that we would be more embraced and not ridiculed. My older sister, Chong, from my mother's previous partner, stood out, but they made sure to give us boys names that Americans wouldn't have difficulty pronouncing or wouldn't find humorous. By giving us names like David and Doug, my parents were trying to assimilate us into an American segregated culture, which systemically had difficulty with interracial marriages and outsiders.

The black-and-white pictures of Mom and Dad together in these early years capture their joy, promise, and hope. Their relationship was strong, their affection for one another tender. Constant kisses and hugs, gentle touches were common in our house. They danced and laughed together constantly. I never saw them argue. Not even a harsh stare or a disappointed glance. Our home felt safe, stable, and filled with anticipation of better things to come. I relished how our family was the envy of so many of my peers. They'd often say, "Man, I wish I had your parents. You're lucky."

In those early years, I could never have imagined how things would change.

My father rarely talked about his childhood, except to share his passion for baseball and fishing. He blossomed as a baseball player and became a good pitcher during high school. We knew that he was born in Missouri and raised in Flint, Michigan, but we didn't know anything about those places. We also knew that he had three older brothers, and that his own father had died of a health condition when Dad was just two years old. He was raised by a single mom, but he never talked about what it was like to grow up without a father. There was never a mention of the extreme poverty he grew up in or the challenges of life without a supportive dad. He rarely spoke about his mom, brothers, or father. But Dad was like my mother in that way. Their childhood and pasts weren't discussed. Right after he graduated from high school, he joined the Air Force and was assigned to the US Eighth Army Compound, Yongsan Garrison, North Post, an American military base in Seoul, South Korea.

"How did you meet Mom?" my sister, Chong, asked him one day.

Dad, sitting in his La-Z-Boy chair near the fireplace in the living room listening to a Joan Baez album, responded: "We met at a party. There were a lot of GIs there. Your mother ran a beauty salon and cut some of the soldiers' hair."

"Did you go up to her or did she come up to you?"

"Not sure about that. But I was wearing a military jacket that I had borrowed from someone, one with a lot of insignias. She thought she was meeting some high-ranking officer instead of just a staff sergeant."

4

Dad chuckled at the memory.

"So what happened when she found out?" Chong asked.

Dad's eyes beamed with humor. "Well, of course, by then she'd already fallen in love with me. I'm sure she must have liked my blue eyes."

When my parents first met, many South Koreans viewed American soldiers as legendary heroes who had rescued them from communism and North Korea's advances. To my mom, my dad was the archetype of the American dream. She never said it in exactly those words, but you could tell by the way she looked at him. The myth of a white knight coming to save the day was real in our family.

Mom also wouldn't talk about her childhood or her past unless we asked. The only details we knew came from her shiny black-lacquered photo album with elegant pearl-encased swans on its cover. Inside were faded black-and-white pictures, some half-torn or cut in half. These photos only made our mother's story more mysterious. They were glimpses of the past, snapshots capturing my mom by a lake laughing or her having fun with friends. We didn't know why other photos were cut in half. We didn't know who were the ones scissored out. We never heard the stories around these pictures. The photos stirred up more questions than answers.

Who does Mom not want to be reminded of anymore? A former lover or partner? A friend?

Did a friend hurt her? Did someone she loved betray her?

We never asked her. We never dug into any potentially juicy stories. We just accepted the mystery. I eventually understood that it's a cultural thing—not talking about the past—especially if it would dishonor or shame the family. We concluded that all was good because nothing was said. There was no need to ask questions because, first, Mom and Dad didn't bring it up, so we surmised it must not be important or relevant. And second, the universe as we knew it was black and white. No need to be focused on the gray, the unknown.

This was a time of great social change, when the religious right was being challenged by the morality of the Vietnam War and in its views on women, abortion, creation theories, the credibility of the Bible, politics, science, and sexuality. In times of challenge like this, polar opposites often become more rigid and hardened. Tribes get more reactive and binary. Life is reduced to right and wrong. Capitalism or communism. Republican or Democrat. Christian or pagan. Conservative or liberal.

At the time, those who had the right answers were the ones typically respected. As I grew older, I found the opposite to be true. Those who asked questions were the ones who were enlightened, challenging the status quo not to be rebellious but because they were thinking.

Our biggest questions weren't about my parents. They were about my sister, Chong. Doug and I knew she was our sister, that she had been born before our parents first met. But none of us knew any details other than that. Chong knew nothing about her birth father, who was never spoken of in our house. Even Chong's name was different than ours. I didn't understand why she didn't have an American name, too. Even Mom had an American name, Debbie. Chong was an unfamiliar name to most Americans, and she frequently became an easy target of jokes.

Growing up, everybody knew who the favorites were in our family. My younger brother, Doug, was Dad's favorite. He was born right after my dad transferred to Japan. Physically, Doug looked most like my dad. He had bigger eyes than Chong and I did. His hair was wavier, like Dad's. His legs were like tree trunks, much like my father. He was cute and adored by my dad. I was Mom's favorite. My siblings and I could tell by the way she looked at me and treated me. Mom would never say it, but we all knew I had a special place in her heart because she couldn't stay upset with me. I think I was irresistibly too cute to her because of my pudgy rolls and triple chin.

Among the three of us, Chong was the responsible one. While my dad cared for her, we could all see he didn't have the same normal familial feelings for her as he had for my brother and me. It seemed that neither of my parents doted on her like they did my brother and me. This didn't change the fact that Mom loved Chong deeply; they shared a special bond that I wasn't aware of when I was a child. Their relationship was forged in suffering from a hidden past, which I wouldn't learn about until much later.

Chong was the super sister. She was a loving child who became a second mom for us while she was still in elementary school. She was quick to care for us. Always looking out for us. Her life wasn't easy. She fed us, babysat us, and made sure we did our homework. And like our mother, Chong quietly performed her responsibilities and remained silent about many things. She always dutifully and meticulously cared for my brother and me. While my mom and dad may have had trouble saying they were proud of us, Chong would frequently give us encouragement, seeing things in us we couldn't see in ourselves.

We were discouraged from speaking Korean as my parents were focused on artfully transitioning us into mainstream American culture. Intermittent Korean words would come up during the normal flow of English when we were referring to food, or in expletives when Mom was upset with us, or when she was talking ear-piercingly loud on the phone with her Korean friends. My parents were concerned that we wouldn't adapt as quickly if we focused on the Korean language. Thank God, because later I found out a lot of my Korean American peers were forced by their parents to attend Korean school on the weekends during Saturday morning cartoons. I would have badgered my parents about that. Looking back, I regret we weren't forced to learn Hangul (the Korean alphabet) because it would have been easier for me to connect to those who are Korean. The lack of

Korean language proficiency foments a shame and sorrow in me that are hard to ignore. My lack of Korean language skills could be interpreted by other Koreans as me not caring about my homeland.

These days, when I meet Koreans who are recently from Korea, the first thing they will ask me is "Do you speak Korean?" I normally respond, "No. Sorry. I didn't learn it as a child. I tried to learn when I was older, but my tutors couldn't stop laughing when they tried teaching me." There was always this compulsion to give a reason why I didn't have mastery over the Korean language. I learned over time not to offer any extended excuse and just say, "No. I wish I did." If Koreans still pursue whether I know any Korean words, I tell them truthfully that the only Korean words I know are the salty profanities, crude toilet words that kids love to giggle about, and of course, the delicious food. But even then, my American pronunciations of Korean words are admittedly humorous. Most of my Korean American friends in defending their own lack of fluency say, "Hey, I speak better Korean than Dave." At least my lack of language competence makes them feel better about themselves.

There was one glorious part of our mom's past that she shared with our family: Korean cuisine. Mom grew up in Jeonju, a city 120 miles south of Seoul. Currently, Jeonju is a popular destination for Korean food lovers and culture seekers. Tourists travel from all over the world to sample its cuisine, especially one of the most notable dishes to come from this region: bibimbap. My wife also loves the other notable Jeonju dish served alongside of bibimbap called Yukoe 육회, the Korean raw beef tartare, a umami-laden, garlicky, cool, nutty, and a little sweet dish.

Mom sometimes made this colorful and healthy dish for us. It begins with cooking rice with beef broth and bean sprouts. Fresh vegetables are artfully positioned around the white fluffy rice in the center: carrots, bean sprouts, radishes, spinach, lettuce, seaweed, pine nuts, and turnips. Then, of course, the ingredients that tastefully combine all the flavors together: gochujang, a hot pepper paste, and a fried egg with a runny yolk.

It was ironic that even though our father served in the Air Force in South Korea, he never developed a taste for Korean food. He loved to mix his white rice with sugar and butter, a habit that's not common to most Koreans I know. It's like putting ketchup on a steak in America.

Korean dishes weren't the most popular meal in our house, however. At that time, TV dinners were the rage. Everything you needed was prepared in prepackaged aluminum-wrapped frozen food trays: beef or fried chicken, potatoes and gravy, corn, and even a cobbler. All you had to do was pop them in the oven. We felt like we were on the leading edge of innovation. This was the late '60s and early '70s. People wanted things faster and more convenient, especially with both parents working all day, as mine were. We loved the processed foods. Corn syrup and plenty of salt covered any abnormalities in the food from this new way of preparation. And in the morning, our cereals were basically colored sugar. Koreans traditionally eat jook for breakfast, a rice porridge with some garlic, onions, mushrooms, and chicken. Simple, elegant, and quite healthy!

At the time, I didn't appreciate how strange it was having bibimbap for dinner one night and then a Swanson Fried Chicken Dinner meal-on-a-tray the next. For the first decade of my life, I didn't know how unique my parents were. Dad and Mom were pioneers, an interracial couple in the '60s. Something that was still illegal in many states. It wasn't until June 12, 1967, that the Supreme Court said it was unconstitutional for states to ban interracial marriages.

I was born at the Yongsan American military base in Seoul, South Korea. While we later lived briefly in Japan after my father got reassigned, my childhood memories are mostly of Greensboro, Maryland, where we settled after my dad left the Air Force. It was a small town, and the social interaction with neighbors was civil, but infrequent. The adults mostly stayed to themselves and out of each other's business, unless they happened to catch each other's eyes or nod while mowing the grass or playing catch with the football in the front yard.

Otherwise, you could live a secluded life. Dad and Mom were mostly grinding away at work or attending required coursework for their careers. While Mom worked on her beautician certificate, Dad focused on a stenographer's certification. They didn't have time to invest in their relational network around the neighborhood. I don't remember seeing other neighbors engage my parents beyond a customary smile or a friendly wave.

Still, my siblings and I felt accepted by everyone. We didn't know there were people who looked at us with condescension. I didn't even realize we were mixed race or that some people saw us as "aliens." There wasn't one racial incident that stood out to me before the fourth grade. I was oblivious to the civil rights movement and the underlying and overt racial tensions happening in America when I was a child. Our parents had created their own ecosystem, which kept us from any noticeable racial hostility. The tensions between the Black community and white people weren't discussed in our house. Interracial relationships were normal. It's what we lived every day.

It wasn't until we left Greensboro, Maryland, several years later that we realized how strange we were to others. How many saw us differently than we saw ourselves. Living in the countryside of Maryland, we were captivated by the wonder of the forests, rivers, lakes, streams, plants, and creatures both large and small. Nature doesn't judge you. You're not worried about how you look when you're romping through the forests or the lush green fields of Maryland and Northern Virginia.

Humans can be different. It's in our primal nature to compare ourselves to others, to judge whether a person is safe or to be feared. To discern whether a person is in or out. A friend or a foe.

The idyllic way I saw life as a child would change. The challenge wouldn't be my language, a foreign accent, my intellect, my ability to understand idioms, or my sensitivity to adapt to normal cultural interactions. It came down to the shape of my eyes.

CHAPTER TWO

Nature Boy

Massive green forests filled with red maples, white oaks, American beeches, and northern red oaks filled my world as I grew up in Maryland. The lush, soaring trees were in abundant supply near our house. They became like friends, silently watching over me, ever present and beaming with life. They felt like they could talk to me. A place of shade from the hot summer sun.

Fresh corn, watermelon, and cherries were frequent treats, mixed, of course, with Korean gimbap, basically a seaweed (gim) rice roll with tasty vegetables and kogi (beef) in the middle. Our town was one of those storybook boyhood places you dreamed about as a child. The best way to describe this place is to call it Narnia from *The Lion, the Witch and the Wardrobe* by C. S. Lewis. It was Narnia because of the wonder I felt. The creatures were new to me and fantastical. And nature itself seemed welcoming with no sense of judgment of who you are.

I was innocent, filled with energy, finding my legs, discovering my potential, running and jumping, traversing all these unknowns, curious, with little fear, thinking the best of people naturally. It was a place where I felt a wild freedom to roam. It was in my blood to run and investigate. I was curious about anything outdoors. I felt like I could create and explore without the worry of lack or others' criticism. With the whole world of Greensboro, Maryland, as my backyard, I felt like I could do anything.

My friends and I spent our time investigating fields, jumping in swamps, riding our bikes for miles, exploring developments as they were being built, or scampering wildly throughout the neighborhoods. Our bikes were our spacecrafts to take us wherever our imaginations wanted to go. We rode our bicycles everywhere. It got more sophisticated when we began using walkie-talkies to communicate with one another. My friends and I entered into nearby construction sites where bulldozers were moving tons of the earth. We'd extract the sticks land surveyors had carefully placed in the ground and use them as swords. The wooden stakes on the construction sites represented future homes. It never crossed our young minds that surveyors had painstakingly positioned them into the ground to mark boundaries and excavation sites.

Penny was our adopted family beagle. We named him after the large brown spot on his short, white furry back. Penny would look at me with those dark puppy eyes like he knew everything I was saying and even what I didn't know how to articulate. Penny and I loved to maneuver our way through nearby fields. Dad would often let him roam unrestrained. When he placed two fingers in his mouth, he blew a loud rising whistle that had an exclamation point, and Penny would race back, knowing his favorite dinner was about to be served.

I loved the forest, the long fields in the rural country and the moist banks of the Choptank River. Birds, dogs, rabbits, deer, frogs, and farms all joyfully interacting in the landscape around us. Lightning bugs, colorful butterflies, and praying mantises were part of the magical world I lived in. The pesky mosquitoes were the enemies. These bloodthirsty insects seemed especially attracted to my Korean blood, an Asian feast they weren't used to. Mosquitoes feasted on me after I'd been in the forest for just a few minutes.

I made so many new discoveries every time I was outside. The evergreen fragrance of the forests; the scent of spring rain; the morning dew; freshly cut Bermuda grass. I'll never forget diving into the ponds by our house, barefoot, splashing in little pools of water with hundreds of tadpoles, hearing the creatures scurrying away from us. If you looked into the sky, you could literally see thousands of birds. A variety of geese, ducks, hawks, and sparrows were flying overhead in tight formations. The quacks, the melodious notes, the distinct sounds of these birds were part of the natural harmony of the area we called home.

The animals were not simply my friends; I felt like I was one of them. Sometimes I would even sing to them. I loved to look out from the patio of our house, where the geese, ducks, and sparrows rested on their migration routes down south. I'd pick up my dad's old guitar, which stood against the wall near the fireplace, then slowly and gingerly open the creaky metal screen door and try not to startle my fowl audience. I'd plop myself on the outdoor lawn chair, position the guitar on my lap, and belt out a nonsensical song to the birds.

Penny would wander onto the deck, and when he'd see the gathering of birds, he'd bolt into the grass after them. Wings would flap and feathers waft as the creatures all tried to escape, some flying and others dashing away. Penny would run around in circles, chasing after them.

I spent so much time outside, my dad started calling me "Nature Boy." Though it probably wasn't just my love of the outdoors that led to this nickname.

Sometimes I'd run in my underwear like some wild animal, my straight black hair protruding from my scalp, sweat running down my face. Dad would burst out laughing watching me, his six-foot athletic frame scrunching up in amusement from my antics. "It's a bird. It's a plane. No! It's Nature Boy!"

I didn't like to wear clothes. Garments inhibited my movement. I wanted to be ready to jump into the nearby natural water holes without hindrance. I followed in my mom's footsteps in this way. While she was going to school to earn her beautician certificate so she could get a license in Maryland, Mom also worked at a factory on an assembly line. When she came home from work, she always took off her beautician outfit, hopped into the shower, and came out with wet hair, wearing no makeup and loose-fitting clothes that often didn't match. If you watch Korean dramas, it's the typical look and vibe of a 할머니 halmoni, a Korean grandma who acts like she owns the town and has the confidence to back it up. A Korean grandma doesn't have to speak; she can just look at you and you know what she is saying. The popularity of Korean dramas is in part because of how authentically expressive the Korean people are beyond words. I can't count how many times I've been quietly pushed aside by a five-foot-tall elderly Korean grandma. Facial expressions and sounds perfectly convey emotions in a shortened code. Like a K-grandma, Mom never cared what others thought, or at least it seemed that way. Other times Mom would come home, shower, and then come out in a casual silk nightie that made her feel comfortable and us uncomfortable. This spirit of freedom was part of my DNA.

"Put a shirt on!" my dad encouraged me, to no avail.

My sister, on the other hand, just groaned. "Ooooh...it's gross seeing your nipples."

I answered the way Mom might have. "I wanna be free."

It would take me a while to be able to articulate that I didn't like feeling confined and restrained by any type of rules. It was ironic, considering how much of my life I spent living by rules. But that was later, after we moved away from Maryland, after everything changed.

My brother, Doug, and I had a daily routine. As soon as we arrived home from school, we raced to the bedroom we shared, lunchboxes and books in hand. The first thing we did was quickly shed our clothes and step into our flannel superhero pajamas. Then we ran to the big box television, plopped ourselves onto the floor, lay down with our hands underneath our faces, and became entranced by the cartoons on the screen. We were the first generation of latchkey kids. The television became our favorite babysitter. Chong, Doug, and I went into a trancelike state watching cartoons. The television was a portal into a new world, like the digital world would someday be to the next generation. When Pong, one of the first computer tennis-like games you played on TV, became part of our world, we thought we'd taken a quantum leap into the future.

One late afternoon, as evening was approaching, Chong started cooking dinner for us, and Doug and I got lost in some animated fantasy on the giant tube. In my peripheral vision, I happened to catch a flickering orange light coming from the kitchen.

"Chong, there's some bright light coming from the kitchen," I said, not thinking much about it. I was mesmerized by the cartoons.

Chong turned her head toward the kitchen and immediately sprang up from her position next to us. Moments earlier, she had heated the oil in a pan for dinner. When she reached the doorway to the kitchen now, she gasped.

"Doug and Dave!" she called out. "We have to leave the house right now! The kitchen is on fire!"

Chong stood by the door, her face pale as if she had just seen a ghost, her eyes full of terror. We jumped up and ran outside. We didn't consider grabbing anything. We were in such shock that we blew right past the hamsters resting in their cage next to the door we burst out of. Thankfully our dog, Penny, followed us outside.

In a matter of moments, the whole front of our house was engulfed in flames. Large, billowing black smoke plumed, polluting the fresh, rural farmland air. I stood in fear, watching the scene unfold as if it were on the evening news. The only difference was I could feel the heat, taste the smoke, and hear the crackling.

The sirens announced the arrival of massive glistening red fire trucks. A fireman jumped off one and unfurled a large hose, then he ran toward the house to extinguish the flames. I looked around us to see neighbors gathering to view the unfolding spectacle.

When Mom and Dad finally arrived, they were relieved to see that we were all safe. We embraced them in disbelief, not saying anything. We didn't know what to say as we watched the frenzy of activity around the house. After the firefighters gained control of the fire, the truth was obvious:

Almost everything we owned was gone.

As our family stood there, stunned, silently, staring at our home in ruins, we thought about everything that was lost. The new furniture that our parents had recently purchased was now destroyed. The beautiful living room sofa that still had its plastic covering on it—ironically, to protect it. The dark coffee tables. Our new television. The beloved stereo system and my dad's prized collection of rock-and-roll music vinyls he had acquired since he was a teenager. My mom's mementos and art collection of gold jewelry. Her ornate boxes and vases made in Korea. So many other priceless objects that held memories from thousands of miles away. All turned to ashes.

I suddenly had a terrible thought.

The hamsters. We forgot the hamsters.

All at once our future had disappeared inside an inferno. The question now was, where would we live?

Chong was never blamed for the fire. She was still a child. My parents weren't cited, either. Life just kept going. We had been renting the house from some farmers, and the landlords kindly let us live with them as our house was being rebuilt. We lived in a trailer on their property for a couple of months, and this pause in my family's life led my parents to reexamine the world we were starting to create in Maryland. They felt like it was time for a change. So did my dad's brother, who lived in Arizona.

"It's a sign from God," Uncle Lloyd told my dad when he found out about the house fire.

My dad's older brother was a stenographer, too, and also a volunteer associate pastor living in Arizona. He had been telling my dad for a while that we should move out there. Some might see this fire as a challenge, but others, like my uncle, viewed it as an opportunity. He encouraged my parents to move to Arizona for a fresh start. We had never even visited Arizona.

I will always give credit to my parents for not freezing in the mess of it all. They had learned how to just move on and make the best of whatever they had in their hands.

Arizona was rapidly growing beyond the typical "snowbirds" coming from the colder climates during the winter months. Now people who wanted to build a new life in the valley of the sun were moving there from all over America. Young families, entrepreneurs, and people looking for their field of dreams streamed into the newly constructed suburbs of the desert in metropolitan Phoenix. Dad and Mom decided to join this new wave of pioneers.

As we left our Narnia to move to the West, Uncle Lloyd was delighted. He would offer us a refuge from our burned-down house in Maryland and even lead us to a place where we could handle the very flames of hell.

CHAPTER THREE

The Valley of the Sun

Seeing the desert for the first time from the backseat in our orange Pontiac Grand LeMans felt like we were on an extraterrestrial space mission. The shapes, huge colorful vistas, and landscapes were captivating. We were accustomed to thick green landscapes, but the desert was all about the stark reality of sand, dirt, cactus, and tumbleweeds. The heat in Arizona can get over 100 degrees in the summer. People say it's different because it's dry heat, but so is a blowtorch. It gets hot enough to fry eggs on the sidewalk.

Arizona would be a dramatic change for my family, and in more ways than just the climate.

We ended up in Tempe, a suburb of Phoenix, home of Arizona State University. Tempe boasted about its independence, its New Age vortexes, and also about how many people had left Southern California to come there for lower taxes and a better opportunity to own a house. Less government, and a vibe of independence. You could feel the future potential of Arizona, with its distinctive desert beauty, chill lifestyle, and relatively low cost of living.

Once we grew accustomed to the summer heat, we loved Arizona. I was only ten years old, but I knew this would be a great place to grow up; my parents felt the same way about uprooting us to Arizona to create a new life. It felt like a place where pioneers could find a home.

Before we'd settled into a new house of our own, we moved in with my uncle and his family. None of us, besides my dad, had ever met them. Uncle Lloyd lived in a three-bedroom house with his wife and three children, and they were hospitable enough to let our family of five live with them. It was a stretch for all of us, but we made it work. What stood out to me was that the backyard contained a bean-shaped, baby blue pool with interwoven cinder blocks as a fence around it.

Uncle Lloyd was the second of four sons, right above my dad. He was born in Sikeston, Missouri, the same place my father was introduced to the world before the family moved to Michigan. During World War II, Uncle Lloyd served in the Army Medical Corps in Europe. Later he enrolled in business college, got married, and attended court reporting school, where he honed his skills as a stenographer like my dad. After becoming a Christian, he enrolled in a Bible college, where he studied to become a pastor.

The first thing I noticed in Uncle Lloyd was his loud, uninhibited, contagious laugh. He was an outgoing man with a constant smile on his face. His icy blue eyes mirrored my dad's. They enlarged every time he laughed. Whenever he said something funny, he scanned the room to see if others were joining in his hilarity. But it didn't matter if others approved or not; if he thought it was humorous, the shoulders on his wiry frame curled as the laughter shook his whole upper body. Watching him get tickled by his own humor was contagious.

One day Uncle Lloyd said, "Hey, David, come here. Come to the bathroom for a second." He had a winsome and innocent way of making people trust him.

I knew he wasn't going to do anything dangerous; people were in the house, and the bathroom door was open. By now I knew he liked to laugh and entertain us, so I followed him into the bathroom without a second thought.

"Watch this," he said.

Uncle Lloyd pointed his index finger and thumb toward his right eye, then in one swooping movement, popped his eye out of his head.

What in the world?

My mouth gaped open. I stopped breathing for a moment. I saw the glass eye he was holding with his two fingers, then I noticed the hollow part of his eye socket with its pinkish flesh and thin blood vessels.

If this is supposed to make me feel more comfortable around you, it's not working.

I offered some form of a smile to be kind, but my uncle just guffawed when he saw my horrified face. He acted like this was the funniest thing he had ever done. But I knew I wasn't the first victim of this family carnival act. It was too well choreographed, so I knew he must have done this to multiple children to see their response.

It's funny how something can look real to you, but you can't unsee it once you discover it's not.

Up to that moment, I had no idea that his right eye was a prosthetic made of hard acrylic. From then on, I never looked at Uncle Lloyd the same way. At dinner, I could feel the queasy sensation in my stomach as I imagined that plastic eye pinched between his thumb and index finger. I never asked him how he lost his eye because I didn't want him to use it as another opportunity to exhibit the new plastic one. I didn't need to know anything more.

This was part of what my dad called "the Gibbonses' warped sense of humor." And aside from this, Uncle Lloyd was endearingly odd yet fun. Ultimately, he was trying to make it through a hard situation. He wasn't going to let the loss of his eye destroy his sense of humor.

One of the hardest things we had to do when we first arrived in Arizona was to give away our family dog, Penny. My uncle didn't want our family dog inside or outside his house. If the shelter couldn't find an owner, they would put her down. Mom gave the shelter extra money to keep Penny much longer than normal. The thought of Penny not being adopted was a possibility we quickly dismissed from our minds.

I found it difficult letting her go. She was a member of our dream team from Maryland. She felt like the last symbol of Maryland that we carried to remind us of where we'd come from. Saying good-bye to Penny made the transition we were making from Maryland to Arizona more final. From a colorful, imaginary world with fantastical creatures to the eye-popping reality of the barren desert. This East Coast–to–West Coast shift was more than geographical.

Soon after we arrived in Arizona, we noticed people staring at us. People just gawked at us like we were exotic animals in a zoo. Stunned expressions. Impulsively, children and even adults squinting or slanting their eyes with their index fingers to try to depict their portrayal of me and my family. They would look at each other and just laugh after trying to mimic our eyes. I soon realized this was the first time many of them had seen an Asian person up close. Some people derisively pointed at us. If some were too timid to make fun of us, we still could see their whispering lips and long stares as we passed them by. I hadn't experienced this in Maryland.

Years later, a group of Asian friends and I walked into a crowded McDonald's restaurant and even then, everyone became quiet. They all looked at us like we had just arrived from Mars. Then a small boy pointed at us, and yelled amid the silence: "LOOK, MOM!"

At the start of fourth grade at a local elementary school, my new classmates peppered me with questions.

"Are you Chinese?" was the first question I always got from kids and parents alike.

If you were Asian when I was growing up, people just assumed you were Chinese. Many people didn't know about Korea.

"No, I'm actually Korean," I answered.

"Where are you from?"

"I'm from Maryland. But if you're asking where I was born— Seoul, Korea, on a US military base."

These were the friendly questions. But the questions soon escalated and turned into more aggressive demeaning attacks: "Chink!" or "Chinaman!" "Go back to your country!" Initially, I tried to avoid the taunts. But after relentless shaming, which was common growing up, it was tough not to respond, especially as I got older.

"I'm not Chinese, bro."

"Well, then, what are you?"

"I'm Korean."

"Okay, you're a Kink!"

As kids laughed, sometimes I tried to laugh, too, acting like this didn't bother me. I didn't want to give anyone the pleasure of thinking their words impacted me negatively. Usually, I just walked away feeling embarrassed and like a freak. They kept making slant eye gestures. At recess and on the bus, in the classroom or in the playground, the ridicule didn't stop, especially as it related to the shape of my eyes. Some were innocuous and innocently curious. Others were more brutal with their incessant racist remarks.

"Hey, can you see through those eyes?" they asked as they tried to physically exaggerate the shape of my eyes on their faces.

"Why is your face so flat?"

"Ahhhh-so. Is that what they say in China to each other?"

"Do you know karate?"

As time went on, the words became more piercing as they tried to mimic a stereotypical Asian immigrant's accent with their voices:

"Hey, Chinaman!"

"You're a chink."

"Gook!"

"Ching Chong!"

This last one had my sister's name embedded in the slur.

The ridicule felt relentless. The worst part was not just hearing the slurs, but knowing what people actually thought even if they weren't saying it out loud. You could see it in their eyes. *The eyes didn't lie.*

It seemed that wherever I went, I was some sort of misfit, the main character of the freak show. I had a running inner dialogue trying to encourage myself.

My eyes aren't shaped upward. Small—yes. Different from everyone around me in Arizona. But they are not slanted eyes. You got this.

Yet, when I was alone, I started pressing the outside edge of my eyes downward to make sure my eyes wouldn't grow upward as I got older. I was hoping I could change the shape of my eyes and stop kids from making me the brunt of their jokes.

For the first time in my life, I began to think that something was inherently wrong with me. That I was less than the white kids I saw around me. Before coming to Arizona, I never even thought about how I physically looked. I don't ever remember being teased. My friendships were all positive. But for the first time, I started thinking about the contours of my eyes and how different I was. And not only different, but what others perceived as ugly or unattractive.

Instead of being awed by the beauty around me, I found myself—without even understanding it—anxious about my personal appearance and what others thought about me. What added to the shame was my portly frame at the time.

One day after I came home from school, I dropped my textbooks in the bedroom I shared with my brother and rushed to the bathroom two doors down the long hallway. All day long, I'd endured criticism about my looks at school, and then on the bus. By now I was highly sensitive to prolonged looks and whispers. I could feel people staring at me without even looking at them. Every time I heard someone laugh, I thought it was about me. The relentless teasing about my appearance had grown into an infinite loop of criticism in my mind.

Standing in front of the mirror, I grabbed the top of my T-shirt and lifted it above my head, tousling my straight black hair in every direction. Then I just stared at my fourth grade self in the mirror. My eyes went to my round midsection, where a couple rolls of fat had continued to grow since I was a baby. Those rolls that were cute on a one-year-old were now noticeably unattractive.

Oh, great. It's not only my eyes. It's my rolls!

How'd I get so plump?

For several moments, I stood there, transfixed. I grabbed my rolls and shook them.

God... why do I have to look this way? Why me? Why?

My self-perception soon became my preoccupation. I was the new alien in Arizona. The Chinaman. The Kink. The easy and cheap laugh for people I didn't know. And I was only in elementary school.

I'd left Narnia behind in Maryland. The world as a place of wonder and endless possibility became a dangerous place of shame and marginalization.

Soon I became more absorbed toward my physical appearance. My creative energy shifted toward proving to people that I was important. My thirst to explore the world turned into a preoccupation with trying to be accepted by others.

This Nature Boy had entered another part of the jungle he hadn't known existed. The easiest way to make yourself feel better is to put someone else down. It's survival of the fittest. It's primal to size people up and draw conclusions. Am I safe? Are they safe? Will they eat my lunch? Can I eat theirs? My childhood imagination of a Disney-like world shifted toward a stark reality of vividly seeing critics and competitors. I learned how to be sharp with my tongue and beat them to the verbal punch.

The house had burned down that year, but so had the innocence of childhood. Yet something even worse began to grow inside me. It was a quiet compliance to the bullying around me. This became clear when a large kid in my neighborhood started mocking my mom.

Ramone, the neighborhood bully, looked and sounded like a grown man even though he was only ten years old. He was the type of kid who needed to start shaving in the fourth grade. He towered over all of us in our elementary school. He was bigger than many of the adult teachers. I heard him making comments not only about me but also about my mom.

"Does she even know English? Why didn't she just stay in her own country?"

My little elementary school self envisioned standing up to Ramone like Bruce Lee in *Fists of Fury*. Bruce Lee was growing in popularity at the time. He tried to do feature films in the United States, but studios rejected him. He decided to go to Hong Kong, where his career took off. Bruce Lee became my generation's hero who helped fight back against Americans' racist attitudes toward Asians. We were characterized as docile, weak, malnourished, asexual, emasculated Asian men. If you were an Asian woman, you were usually sexualized, considered exotic, or demeaned. Most of us were just trying to "assimilate." To become absorbed into the great white matrix.

Many people, not just white people, struggled with accepting the uniquenesses of Asians—or anyone who was not like them. Being an "other" in America was something the Black community had dealt with for centuries, and the growing group of "yellows" and "Orientals" also experienced racism, stereotyping, and marginalization. This was hardly new for Asians in America. Asians had been used and abused to build the railroads in America. They were the victims of hate crimes and discrimination. Whole families with children were sent to internment camps during World War II, where during that period of forced encampment they lost homes, businesses, farms and other properties, and jobs. There are records validating the abuse, trafficking, and even slavery of Asians in America. But as our numbers grew, so, too, did the comments, slurs, and overt racism, along with the calls to assimilate.

Bruce Lee, however, wasn't having it. He was the embodiment of an attractive, muscular, strong Asian hero with a no-nonsense attitude toward people who looked down on Asians. In the midst of this assimilation focus was someone who embraced his unique identity. Bruce Lee *didn't* want to assimilate. He integrated yet stayed true to himself.

For young Asian kids who didn't see anyone like them on television or in starring roles at the theater, Bruce Lee was iconic. He offered hope for a rising group of Asians who felt out of place in America. He embodied the opposite of how I felt as a child in Arizona. He was strong, confident, calm, and cool. He wouldn't walk away from the racism he faced. He challenged it and overcame it.

I loved to imagine standing before Ramone and facing him like Bruce Lee. Before Ramone moved, I would launch a simple kick to his chest and leave an imprint of my sneaker on his shirt while he flew straight through a window. But as much as I dreamed of standing up to Ramone, the reality was that I was afraid of him. I'd seen him fight at school; the guy was brutal. Regrettably, I never challenged him, not even when he brazenly mocked my mom directly to my face. I cowered in fear.

There are moments in life when you wish you spoke up. I was silent with Ramone that day but that embarrassing moment prepared me for a group of people who would teach me how to fight.

CHAPTER FOUR

Fists of Fury

The biggest adjustment we made after moving to Arizona wasn't transitioning into a new house. It came when we began to attend church for the first time. Uncle Lloyd's hope all along had been to bring us to his local church, where he served as a part-time pastor. We never went to church before we moved to Arizona, so I knew nothing about God or Jesus or Muhammad or Buddha. If anything, my family was agnostic. My parents felt a bit obligated to go to Uncle Lloyd's church since we were staying at their house. Religion wasn't a part of our life, but it was about to become one. A very significant part.

On the first Sunday we visited, I spotted a sign that read "City Baptist Church: an Independent, Militant, Fundamentalist Baptist Church." City Baptist and other churches like it were known as the "Fighting Fundamentalists." I was too young to understand what these adjectives meant, but that branding was all over the church. I figured that if the people at Uncle Lloyd's church were anything like Uncle Lloyd and his family, it couldn't be all that bad. Maybe weird, but I figured they were the salt of the earth, good-natured, transplanted Midwesterners and East Coast people. When you go to a church that describes itself in this way, it should tell you a lot, but we were fresh from the East Coast and simply trying to make friends and adapt to our new desert environment. Besides, these were Uncle Lloyd's friends.

Uncle Lloyd introduced our whole family to his Christian subculture of mostly blue-collar hardcore fundamentalist believers. It was its own world within the real world. A physical prelude to the metaverse. This was a religious alternative reality that felt familiar and safe because Uncle Lloyd was one of the leaders. The members of the church made us feel welcome. Not only did they see us, but we even had some insider favor because we knew Uncle Lloyd. City Church was helpful in getting our family connected to the area. The people made it feel like home. They were warm and accepting. The racist overtones I felt in the new public school were less common at this church.

When we moved into our new house, we thought we were living the dream: we had the kidney-shaped pool, new cars, and a beautifully furnished home. The young people of our church loved coming to our house to swim and eat our barbecued chicken, hot dogs, and hamburgers. We were considered cool and rich by the congregants who knew us. For the first time, I felt people envy my situation.

Mom quickly became well loved and popular at the salon nearby. She became the one making it financially rain for the owner of the salon. Mom would wake up around 5 a.m. and come back home between 5 and 6 p.m. She was always hustling. She didn't have time to prepare meals, so she bought us TV dinners in shiny aluminum trays. If we were lucky, she'd bring home a bucket of KFC with all the sides of mashed potatoes, cole slaw, and biscuits.

We loved our new house, but we ended up finding a home at our church. We were genuinely excited about going to the services. For a family that had been primarily left to ourselves in Maryland, entering this new church community was exciting. My hardworking parents started hosting pool parties and gatherings at our house on weekends. Many of the others in this church community also considered themselves outsiders. They believed they were a minority group of people taking a "narrow" road that others in the world wouldn't take. They were willing to suffer ridicule and abuse for their beliefs. Their mission was to be holy and separate from the world. Their passion was to see people saved from their sins and to help others know about the way to get to heaven. My dad and mom, who had always enjoyed a good party, had to reorient themselves to this new standard. My dad was directed to give up cigarettes if he was going to try to follow Jesus and abstain from "worldly" things. It was a cultural shift, but they had already made major adjustments as an interracial and intercultural couple. They knew how to adapt. We never saw them struggle with new settings or people. They could be the life of the party or let others shine. Dad's only struggle with the rules in this church was the no smoking thing. Dad would secretly go to the alley behind our home to smoke. We knew where he hid his cigarettes. They were on this high shelf in the bathroom he thought we couldn't reach. It was one of his few vices that we were aware of.

We soon got used to spending our whole Sundays at church. There were Sunday school classes before or after the services. Seeing "school" in the church bulletin was enough to give me hives. Why would any kid want to do "school" again on a Sunday? And then sitting through long services where they played an organ and sang old songs you'd never heard before? Add a speaker reading the Bible in what sounded like another language and who tells you if you don't know Jesus, you're going to hell? It definitely took some getting used to.

But my parents got "saved" (meaning that they were rescued from hell) and so did us kids. In fact, I got saved quite a few times. I was wearing the carpet out, walking up and down the aisles of the church whenever a speaker said we needed to come forward to accept Jesus so we wouldn't go to hell. I felt embarrassed to keep taking the speakers up on their invitation, but my shame didn't seem like too much to bear compared to spending an eternity in hell.

As a fourth grader, I'd run forward during the invitation after the pastor had given his message. I could feel the flames of hell torching my derriere. Every invitation was a chance to either become saved or rededicate my life to Jesus. Occasionally, they would invite us to serve God with our whole lives by choosing to become a missionary or pastor. That was the Holy Grail. Those who accepted this call were all in. Usually, an old hymn like "Just as I Am" was played multiple times. You would usually have a good five to ten minutes to respond. Every Sunday this would happen, in the morning and in the evening. Sometimes these come-to-Jesus moments happened in Sunday School, too, and anytime we had revival meetings.

"Let's sing one more stanza," the pastor would say. "Maybe there's one more soul that's ready to come." "If you have any shadow of a doubt you're not a Christian, you come now." That phrase, 'shadow of a doubt,' got me every time. I had doubts all the time.

Sure, maybe this was just a ploy to give people more time to come up for the altar call. But time after time, I'd feel compelled to go up before the last stanza was sung. The speakers were so passionate and emotional that I couldn't help but be swayed—or more accurately, terrified. I probably walked forward or said the same prayer in my seat at least a hundred times during these invitations. I wasn't convinced my soul was saved.

We were also introduced to revival meetings. Revivals were special meetings held on Sundays and throughout the week. Visiting evangelists came with captivating, polished, well-rehearsed, riveting, and dramatic messages. Our church said we couldn't go watch Hollywood movies because of their "worldly" influence on us, so this was the next best thing. We'd cry and we'd laugh. Give money and make decisions to do more and be better. These meetings would fuel the growth of our new family church. They were Sunday services on Red Bull. We were encouraged to bring our friends so that they, too, wouldn't go to hell. Who needed televisions and theaters? We had all the drama we needed in church. The messages were usually very theatrical and entertaining. You'd cry and laugh the whole time.

Revival meetings could be from 7 p.m. to 10 p.m. every night of the week during certain seasons of the year. The service began with a kind welcome to everyone, then a few hymns. Special music followed, by either a group or an individual. Then different evangelists came in and talked about hell or the sins that we had been committing, like pride, anger, fighting, and thinking too many lustful thoughts. They also worked to convince us that we were living in the last days before Jesus would return to judge the world. The speakers prophetically declared an apocalyptic nightmare for most people after Jesus returned. But if you were a Christian, you had a golden ticket out. You would be taken up to heaven in an event called "the Rapture." A Star Trek–like event where millions of people would be beamed up into the presence of God. You didn't want to be left behind for what came after the Rapture—it would basically be endless torture. If you got left behind, hell on earth was awaiting you.

During one of the nighttime revivals, the special music was performed by The Inspirations. They were a group of young women with long, iron-curled hair that was feathered back and hair-sprayed meticulously into place. They wore long dresses they had sewn themselves, because that way they could be sure to stay within the standard of the appropriate length of skirts not dependent on "worldly" clothing designers. No skirts could rise above the knees. My sister, Chong, joined the group. Four white girls and Chong, who was the only Korean young woman in the church until one of the members of the church adopted two Korean girls. On this night they sang a song called "I Wish We'd All Been Ready." Another name for it could have been "Night Terrors." If you didn't have a night terror before, just listen to this song one time. The backdrop is guns, wars, and people getting trampled on the floor wishing they had said yes to Jesus when they had an opportunity. And then the constant refrain:

There's no time to change your mind,
the Son has come

[dramatic pause]

and you've been left behind.

They sing this in perfect harmony, with perfect smiles, not at all concerned.

This song would give me nightmares for years.

Am I really going to be raptured?
What about my family and friends?
And how about the people who don't believe like us?
Are we living in the end times?

And to be honest, I didn't want Jesus to return quite yet. I wanted to get married and have kids first. And I wanted to have sex before Jesus came back. But I couldn't say that out loud, because I was taught that marriage and sex are nothing in comparison to being with Jesus.

That's a hard sell to a teenager. Sunday school teachers would say that marriage doesn't compare. I would think, *Easy for you to say, bro, since you're already married.*

After the smiling young women made their way back to their seats in the front row, the evangelist strode up to the podium to deliver a message that built on the fears provoked by this song. As the sermon crescendoed, he spoke dramatically, often in a quiet, haunting tone. You could hear a pin drop.

"If you don't accept Christ, you are destined to go to hell. You're in complete darkness. The hottest heat in the world is a black heat. Bumping into people you don't know. Never seeing anybody. In constant pain and terror. But you don't have to be left behind. You don't have to go to hell if you die, because if tonight you accept Jesus to be your God, you can have eternal life. Come forward now as the pianist plays 'I Surrender All.' Don't wait; you come now. Friend, don't be left behind."

The dramatic speakers weren't the only ones who inspired dread and despair inside me. We were given a best-selling book called *666* by Salem Kirban, and inside were black-and-white photos depicting what it would be like in the last days. The photographs shared in the book were taken from the Holocaust to convey what this end-time scenario would look like.

I had nightmares about being left behind for years. I would wake up from one of those dreams, my heart elevated, my breathing shortened, and eyes wide open. Grateful that I was alive and there was still time left for me to make sure once again I was "saved." Once I even came home to find nobody home and I instantly panicked, thinking I'd missed the Rapture. Eventually I found my brother, and at first I was relieved. But then I remembered who my brother was and assumed we'd both been left behind!

I laughed at my panic, but then my laughter quickly subsided because I wouldn't want even my worst enemy to go through the period of time that would be called the Tribulation. We were told life and everything in the world would continue to get worse. Eventually the end of humanity would come and Jesus would rescue us by coming again. We were convinced that the only reason we were on this planet was to share Jesus with someone so they wouldn't have to experience the end times or eternal hell. As a child, I was trained to go door to door in the new neighborhoods in Arizona to share the good news. Our youth group would either place paper tracts advertising the church on doors or canvas the neighborhood, knocking on doors and engaging the unsuspecting homeowners.

"Hi, my name is Dave and these are my friends. We're from City Baptist Church. If you don't mind, could we ask you a question?"

Most of the people were kind, just smiled and awkwardly took the tract or little pamphlet we handed to them. I imagine many of them threw the handouts into the trash can. But if they were interested and said we could ask them a question, we kept going with the script we'd memorized and delivered the stilted, robotic and awkward pitch:

"Sir, if you were to die tonight, do you know where you would go? Heaven [*hand gesture points to the sky*] or hell [*hand points to the ground*]?"

If they said heaven, we asked them how they knew. If they said some version of, "By believing in Jesus that he died and came to save us, and asking him to forgive us of all our sins and accepting his gift of eternal life," then we were satisfied that they were indeed "saved." If not, then we showed them what the answer was by way of diagrams and Bible verses.

Embarrassed, I still knocked on doors with these pink paper tracts, but we were trained to work through that reluctance. If these people died and went to hell, we were told, then one day they might ask us a haunting question:

"Why didn't you tell me?"

As I look back on this, much of what we did was motivated by fear. For years, I got off planes feeling guilty for not speaking to the person sitting next to me about Jesus. This mind-set taught me to look at people as projects. It was robotic and felt unnatural. It felt cold, because there wasn't the natural flow of respect, because it wasn't about having compassion for others but essentially just preaching at people.

Later in my life I read in the Bible that "perfect love casts out fear." The Jesus I read about seems to fiercely love everyone—especially those who don't know him or would be considered the worst of sinners. Jesus seemed to love the outcasts, the misfits, the marginalized, and those considered outside the norm. In the Christian bubble I grew up in, we said Jesus loves people. But I don't remember that feeling dominating me as much as fear and the urgency to get people "saved." That was our common agenda whenever we met someone new.

Our training was that if you were not "saved," you were still thinking like the world and living like the world (the "world" being defined as a culture not of God, one that was opposed to and even hostile to a Christian's beliefs and value system). Which then meant that you were foolish in your thinking. Not to be trusted. A possible "wolf in sheep's clothing." People were souls to be won, fish to be caught, or wolves who would prey upon us if we didn't watch out. People who weren't Christians were not respected as much as those who were Christians. If you'd asked us, we would have said that all people were made in God's image, but there was a world of a difference between the way we treated those who were Christians and those who were not. If someone wasn't "saved," you couldn't trust their thinking, logic, worldviews, or presuppositions. There was a clear us-versus-them mind-set. Saved and unsaved. You're either in or you're out.

Our mission became clear. The reason we were left on the earth was to witness to others. Expect those liberals and worldly people to be against you. Hang in there—Jesus is coming soon even if most of the world is going to hell. And this was the good news.

CHAPTER FIVE

Saved by a Short-Haired Jesus

When the bell went off at 8:29 a.m., my classmates and I stopped the small talk and messing around on the playground and hurried to get in line for opening assembly. Kids scrambled to get in place. It was the first bell of two; when the second campus bell rang, we were all expected to be in neat rows, much like you'd see at a military academy. We all lined up according to our grades outside on the asphalt parking lot. This was the protocol every morning before the start of our classes.

I was at a new school. My parents became more comfortable with our church, and they'd made the decision to send Doug and me to the newly formed Christian school called City Academy, which was conveniently located five minutes from our house. This was my opportunity for a fresh start. This school had been started by City Church, so to the delight of my uncle Lloyd, we were now immersed into God things almost 24/7. Doug and I were at church and the school almost every day of the week. We spent more time at church than at Uncle Lloyd's house. There was chapel or church services every day. Bible classes, too.

Chong didn't have to attend our private school because they didn't have high school classes available yet. So she stayed at the public school in Mesa, Arizona. But Doug and I were excited because attending private school felt like we were moving on up in the world. It was like we had even achieved a new economic status. Only the rich kids went to private schools. We felt like our parents were making bank.

In actuality, the school leaders were less concerned with providing an elite customized education and more concerned with making sure we children weren't indoctrinated with "worldly" thinking. The focus for the school was biblical teaching to counter the public school's "heresies." When school started, they didn't have teachers for some of the grades. They had room monitors who gave us booklets to read and administered tests. It was a form of do-it-yourself education—they called it self-learning.

City Academy had a smaller student body than the public school, so each student could get customized care, even if the teachers weren't credentialed. The "teachers" were diligent to make sure we were law-abiding citizens. The environment felt safer because there were strict rules. But it could feel oppressive if you were used to more fun environments. Rules existed about everything—clothing, profanity, hairstyles, music, movies, and respect for authority. Boys had to make sure their hair was cut off by their ears and tapered in the back. This was an annoying rule because long hair was more in vogue. As we were becoming teenagers, our looks and fashion mattered. One day I asked a school leader about this rule. I was perturbed about it, but trying hard not to sound disrespectful.

"Why do we have to get such short haircuts?"

Even before he answered, the leader's annoyed expression telegraphed exactly how he felt.

"Isn't it obvious? It's because Jesus had short hair. Long hair is a sign of rebellion. Also, read this pamphlet about how historically it's been noted he had short hair."

Jesus had short hair?

I had assumed Jesus had long hair. All the pictures I'd seen depicted Him with long flowing dark hair. He was white and even had blue eyes. I didn't challenge the teacher at the time; I wasn't able to muster up the courage. Besides, we were taught to simply respect authority. Don't argue. They made sure to tell us that the Bible says rebellion is worse than witchcraft.

I later understood that the long hair rule was really about their belief that the culture's embrace of long hair was an expression of rebellion. At the time, the US government was making multiple blunders, especially as it related to the Vietnam War. A rising number of young people were tired of seeing their friends and classmates sent into combat for what they felt to be a needless war, and they grew their hair long in protest or simply because it looked good long. Our teachers told us the Christian response:

"We're not to have this type of spirit of rebellion against our government. The Bible says we are supposed to render the things that are Ceasar's to Caesar. Unless, of course, it conflicts with the Bible" (meaning their interpretation of the Bible).

While the boys had to consider hair length, the girls had to ponder skirt lengths, since miniskirts were in style. The girls had to wear long dresses reminiscent of television Westerns or skirts that didn't go above the knees. Pants weren't allowed, either, because you couldn't look like the boys. Pants were to be worn only by boys and men, even during the physical education classes. The only trousers the girls could wear during this period were hybrid pant skirts called culottes. Unfortunately for the girls at our school, the required culottes were an ugly shade of green. It was odd that they couldn't wear shorts. Again, that would be considered "worldly" for showing too much skin.

Each day at City Academy started the same. At the morning assembly, our principal greeted us in his crisp white shirt, dark tie, and dark suit coat and quoted a Bible verse. Two students would then be selected to hold the Christian flag and a large black Bible. We placed our hands over our hearts and recited three pledges first to the American flag and then to the Christian flag. The latter was mostly white with a blue square like the American flag, but instead of stars, a red cross was placed in the middle of the blue square.

After the pledge to the American flag, we still had our hands over our hearts.

"I pledge allegiance to the Christian Flag and to the Savior for whose Kingdom it stands. One Savior, crucified, risen, and coming again with life and liberty to all who believe."

Then the students all stared at the individual who held the bible, and we continue on:

"I pledge allegiance to the Bible, God's Holy Word, I will make it a lamp unto my feet and a light unto my path and will hide its words in my heart that I might not sin against God."

Throughout the day, the Bible was taught and spoken about. If we memorized verses, we were rewarded with stickers and prizes. And of course, admiration from parents and leaders. Insignias were placed on our gray uniforms for memorizing verses and chapters of the Bible. I came to discover that the evangelical world often used warlike imagery and nomenclature. We sang songs with lyrics like:

Onward Christian Soldiers
marching into war
with the cross of Jesus
Going on before.

Later, at my Christian college, the ministerial class at our large assembly would sing:

Souls for Jesus is our battle cry,
souls for Jesus we'll fight until we die.

Even the gray uniforms we were wearing in these church kids' clubs were modeled after military uniforms. We were instilled with the belief that life is a war against Satan and the world.

Furthermore, the Bible was the primary way God spoke to us. Everything that was of importance to guide us in life could be found in the Bible. The Bible was revered. Not only was the Bible considered inspired and inerrant, but the translation needed to be the 1611 King James version, which sounds Shakespearean. Other translations of the Bible were considered too liberal and again labeled "worldly." The Bible was of such reverence to our subculture of Christians that Scriptures were weaponized to combat moral issues we thought others were wrong about. We were taught that there was only one way to interpret the Scriptures: the way our local church interpreted them. Others outside of our interpretation of the word of God were labeled liberals or compromisers, lukewarm people God wanted to vomit out of His mouth. I would later learn if you didn't agree with certain beliefs about women, or associated with people of different theological positions on abortion, race, divorce, or the gay community, you could basically be excommunicated. They called it the doctrine of separation, where you would not be included in the community anymore.

Our academy also taught us that to be a Christian meant you were loyal and submissive to your country, the church, and the Bible. While I never heard it stated outright, the growing sentiment at the church was that to be Christian was to be Republican. Republicans affirmed our biblical beliefs about certain issues through their political platforms: fiscally conservative, small government, low taxes, pro-guns, pro-life, pro–death penalty, anti-LGBTQ, anti-feminist. The Republican Party found its home among our conservative Christian community. God and country went hand in hand. We were told to "submit to government authorities for there is not an authority that God does not establish," especially if they were pro-life, pro-guns, anti-taxes, and anti–gay marriage. Our manual to live this life was the Bible and our particular interpretation of it. We took the Bible as the absolute, inspired Word that was breathed from the mouth of God. Man's opinion didn't matter—except, of course, what we believed was our biblical interpretation. The attitude was if you don't believe the way we do, don't let the door hit you on the way out. Oh, and we love you in the Lord.

This marriage of God, country, and the Bible became the root of what we know as Christian nationalism today. To be Christian is to be American. The vision is to make our nation more like God's kingdom. Elect Christian leaders and vote for a Christian agenda primarily advocating for our views of sexuality, schools, abortion, guns, and Supreme Court justices. In the mix of all this—though perhaps not as blatant—were our church's opinions of race and diversity. If we don't believe in interracial marriage and you're married interracially, are you still really one of us? Or are you now a liberal, a worldly one going down that slippery slope? The church I grew up in didn't openly question my parents' interracial marriage, but looking back now, I know it would have been different if my mom or my dad had been Black.

Over the years I didn't question this much, but as I neared my teenage years, I mustered up the courage to talk to the senior pastor at our church, a man the size of an offensive tackle on a college football team. His shoulders were wide; he was tall in stature, intelligent, well spoken; and he had an authoritarian presence. Most of the time he wore an array of nicely tailored suits. He parted his hair on the left side and it was slicked back, nicely combed.

"Dr. Simpson, is it true everything in the Bible is so black and white?" I asked.

He was serious as he looked down at me and smiled.

"Yes, son. There is no gray in the Bible."

He said this with absolute confidence and assurance. He believed this. For years, this would be my stance as well: black and white, no gray. It's nice to be so clear on things. To have an answer for almost everything. You learn to submit to leaders and not question them. At the time, I was starting to have more questions about the beliefs and values that we were told were biblical. Yet soon, events in my life would come where this type of boundary setting would be comforting to me.

And even though I wasn't sure about all the "truth" I was being taught, I did have a group of friends whom I loved in this community and I knew they cared for me. Our friendship has weathered a lot of storms. This is an unusual group of friends because I know that even though I have different views on issues that matter to them, they still remain friends.

Difficult storms were coming, and I would need them.

CHAPTER SIX

Origin Stories

You'll often hear Koreans talking about jeong. It's a word layered with meanings about love, affection, loyalty, and bonding. It describes a strong, soulful loyalty deeply embedded in the Korean people. It's a connectedness to both people and places, and can go deeper than friendship or even love. It's a magical connection that grows with time and shared understanding and experiences.

I didn't know how to describe it when I was young, but it was part of my Korean roots. We kids could feel it. One way we felt her deep love, her jeong for us, was when Mom took us shopping. While Mom would act like she didn't care for us, she would shamelessly brave unfamiliar social norms to make sure we were provided for.

"We're going shopping," Mom would say. She liked to take us to the local shopping center called the Fiesta Mall. On one such outing, Mom decided to buy us matching outfits for Easter. We ended up with faddish leisure suits, 100 percent polyester. The lapels were huge, and the floral silk shirts had collars that resembled airplane wings. If you turned a certain way while wearing them, it felt like the wind might possibly lift you off the ground. Doug had an orange suit, while mine was baby blue. I tried to be cool and unbuttoned the shirt a couple more notches lower than normal from the collar, though being young and Asian, I had no hair on my chest to show off.

Since I was still a bit chubby, Mom went to a certain section in the boys' department of the store to buy my clothes. When I saw the description of the clothing, I wanted to run in the opposite direction. "Husky." *She's buying me husky pants.* Already conscious of my Asian eyes, now I was going to be wearing the clothes of another subset of America that was made fun of: chubby boys.

Mom never ceased to embarrass me. On this particular shopping day, she went to the husky section and asked the clerk the price of a shirt.

"Ma'am, it's twenty dollars," he said.

With a smirk on her face and all her charisma flowing, she glowingly said, "Okay, I'll give you fifteen."

I tugged at her arm. "Mom. You can't do this. This isn't Korea. You don't bargain in America at department stores."

Whenever she did something like this, the salesperson either looked totally befuddled or they laughed, thinking it was cute that she was so audacious. I just knew I did not want to be there with her embarrassing me like that.

Mom, however, didn't mind. We were invisible at this point. She ignored any of our sighs or sounds of embarrassment.

Another time, something set her off. I don't remember what it was, but Mom got tickled by something and started laughing. She laughed so hard that she eventually folded forward, started shaking, and then rolled onto the floor, overcome by laughter. She would often laugh this way at home, but in the middle of the largest shopping mall in our city? I bolted as far away from her as I could get, trying to be incognito. I didn't want people to think we were related. But it wasn't hard to deduce that we were all family; after all, we were the only Asians in the mall.

While I was hypersensitive, always trying to blend in, Mom was the exact opposite. Somehow, she had learned not to care. She knew she was unique. She owned her anomaly status. She was ahead of her time in fashion. She could wear things that didn't match and still look cool.

My childhood self didn't realize that this was what made my mom so refreshingly unique. She was an iconoclastic Korean immigrant, irreverent of customs. Mom became a model for us on how to be yourself without fear of public criticism or need for approval. She knew who she was. She already had to go through the gauntlet of societal scrutiny that categorizes you based upon your education, family, friends, titles, and material possessions, and she just didn't care.

This was never more evident than at the buffet. Sundays after church were all about feasting. We would head on over to the best buffet restaurant near our house, called Royal Fork. It was the most economical place to take the Gibbons boys as we were growing into manhood. We were buffet experts. After filling our trays and finding our tables, we could sequester ourselves there for hours. With great pride, my brother and I saw how many empty plates we could stack up. I think my mom was even prouder.

The buffet line was like a classical music concert to us. Where the concerto might start off slow and soft, what awaited you at the end was the glorious crescendo of music that left you breathless and fully satisfied. Pass on the stuff like Jell-Os and salads up at the beginning of the buffet line. Those who were well versed in buffet culture knew you left room on your plates and space in your stomachs for the most expensive and tastier items at the end of the buffet line. At the end of the buffet line were fried chicken and then, the very last item, the glorious, mouthwatering, juicy prime rib. Awaiting you at the end of the buffet line was the Maestro, who was most likely a high school senior making minimum wage, but he looked good. With a white chef's hat and a white chef's jacket bloodied by the meat, a knife in one hand as well as a large carving fork in the other, he'd look at you, smile, and say, "Sir, would you like prime rib today?"

Trying to act calm, I'd smile, hold out my plate, and say, "Of course! And could I have an extra slice, too?"

My brother and I were both in training—me for football, Doug as a bodybuilder and karate master. We could consume massive amounts of food. We would have fun stacking our plates after each trip to the buffet line. We were determined that the buffet ownership would lose money on us.

After two hours of constant consumption, I would then do a very Korean thing. When you were full to the brim, you unbuttoned the top of your pants and, if necessary, pulled down your zipper slightly so that the inflated size of your belly could comfortably breathe and pop over the waistline of the pants.

As we were chilling in a food stupor with our buttons open and our zippers slightly down, Mom would get up quietly and head to the buffet line. She'd take a plate. Proceed to the end of the line and pile her plate up with fried chicken. Then she came back to our table. Ignoring the looks from other diners and staff, Mom would slowly unfold a large paper dinner napkin on her lap, then elegantly and neatly place all the fried chicken on it.

We'd all want to hide.

"Mom—the sign says you can't take food home!"

Once again, she never said anything. She acted like she didn't hear us. She would proceed to gently enfold the chicken in the napkin and then place the whole bundle of contraband into her purse. We'd roll our eyes and tell her how she was embarrassing us.

But later when we got home, my brother and I always ate the

chicken straight out of the napkin, grinning at each other with crumbs on our faces, licking our fingertips.

We just thought Mom was trying to save money. Mom worked so hard, and her superpower was saving money. She would consistently save enough money to purchase a new car for my father every couple of years. And Mom loved buying us new clothes. With an eye for fashion, her outfits were always colorful and in vogue. Yet despite her love for fashion, I noticed how Mom spent most of her money on our clothes rather than on her own. She had so much joy in giving us things she never had growing up.

At the time, none of us could have imagined the conditions she lived under as a child that made her want to save money yet be so generous to her children. She would get anything for us. To my mom, a few odd looks at the mall or the cafeteria were nothing compared to what she had physically, emotionally, and psychologically endured all her life. She never seemed concerned how people stared at us or made fun of us. She'd stay silent about others' opinions about us. She knew it wasn't something she could control, but more important, she had dreams for us, and she wasn't going to let a few stares get in her way.

Up to that point, Mom had never spoken to us about her childhood years, but one day she surprisingly explained to my sister about her past. Later, Chong told Doug and me the details of this conversation. In Korean, Chong sounds similar to the word "jeong," and especially after hearing this story, I think it is the perfect name for my sister.

Mom loved Chong deeply; they had a special bond, and while my brother and I had been wrapped up in getting accustomed to the new private school and making friends, I didn't notice how lonely my sister felt. Mom had been watching Chong feel progressively more out of place in our home. She was the one "adopted" by my dad, although biologically related to my mom. It never meant anything

49

to Doug or me; we always saw her as our sister. But Chong felt like a perpetual outsider. She hadn't been given an American name. She also felt distant from our father. He would tease her about her looks while also being stricter with her. Seeing Chong's emotional struggle with who she was as a freshman in high school, Mom decided it was the right moment for a deep, heart-to-heart conversation with Chong.

"Chongae. Come on. Let's go sit and talk." (This two-syllable version of Chong's name is the correct pronunciation. When Mom would get affectionate, she would call my sister Chongae. Mom shorted her name to Chong only because it was easier for Americans to understand and pronounce.)

After they went into the living room and sat down on the couch, Mom looked deeply into Chong's eyes and tears started to fill her own eyes. She held both of Chong's hands.

"Chong, I think it's time I tell you more about your 아버지 abuhji/father."

Mom began by talking about her own childhood.

"When I was little, I witnessed my dad getting drunk. You know many Korean men drink heavily because they've had a hard life. They don't know what to do with their pain, especially after the Korean War. So many of us were very poor. We had to eat things that Americans would never eat unless they were starving like us. During the Korean War, I remember running outside the house and hiding because of the bombs that were bursting loudly around us. I would hide in fear."

Chong held on to each word Mom said.

"Your 할아버지/hal-abuhji/grandfather would come home after drinking and then beat your 할머니 halmoni/grandmother," Mom continued. "Then he would be abusive to me as well. My father died of toxic alcohol syndrome. Eventually when I was about sixteen, I ran away from home. I knew I couldn't survive there. I fell in love. I started living with a Korean ROK soldier. And Chong—you were born of that love. You may be surprised, but I had already been pregnant two other times and lost both babies. You were the one beautiful gift to come out of our relationship. Your father was a good man, but like your grandfather, when he got drunk, he would become another person. I tried staying with him, but when I had you, I was afraid for you. Who would care for you if he accidentally killed me? I started thinking, 'What home is this for my daughter to live in?' I gave him an ultimatum that he had to stop drinking, and he promised he would because he loved me and he loved you. But he didn't stop. So I ran away with you."

Mom continued, "Your father found me again. I told him he had one more chance but he continued to drink and be abusive. One day when he passed out, I took you and whatever I could take with me and ran away one last time. Since then, I've never seen nor talked to him. Those pictures you see in the family photo album that are cut in half, some of them are of your father.

"Chong, you came from that complex relationship. But you were always loved, even by your birth daddy. Gary, your father now, adopted you. But you're from me. You're my princess. I always wanted a little girl, so you were a dream fulfilled. Gary loves you, too. I know it hasn't been easy for you to come to America, taking care of your brothers. You've been so brave. You saved your brothers' lives from the fire in Maryland. Now look at how beautiful you are. I love you, Chongae. I promise I will always be here for you."

Mom then took her pinky finger and wrapped it around Chong's pinky finger. The promise of love and that Mom's care for her would never cease. In Korean culture, making a promise by linking pinky fingers is called son-mool (손물), which literally means "finger water" or "hand water." Breaking a pinky promise is considered a serious breach of trust. Mom then just held Chong, and Chong embraced Mom tightly. She laid her head on Mom's shoulder and wept.

A comforting voice sometimes woke me up in the middle of my dream. In the quiet dark of early morning, my dad would nudge me as his low voice whispered my name. I didn't mind climbing out of bed and getting ready. I knew where we were going.

My dad enjoyed taking Doug and me fishing. He meticulously prepared for these fishing excursions, getting together the poles, the bait, all the accessories, extra fuel, and even lunch. He'd wake us up early and we'd drive over an hour to Canyon Lake, a place surrounded by red rock canyon walls and full of hidden coves. There we would fish for bass and trout, and in the process might see a bighorn sheep or deer wander close to shore.

Before we upgraded to a nice bass boat, Dad only had this twelve-foot metal boat with no motor. He'd set up the rack on the roof of his car and hoist the boat all by himself, since we were too small at the time to offer him any real assistance. When we arrived at the lake, he'd put the large metal boat on his back and carry it down to the water himself. His feet would slip going down the precarious, rough, rocky slopes leading down to the lake. Once the boat was in the water, he had to bring all the equipment and food on board. It was a major undertaking for one person, and was made worse by two suburban boys allergic to work.

I have great memories of being out on the lake, floating on the beautiful black-green water. When Dad felt we weren't catching fish, he'd row us around the lake to let us troll. For me, it really didn't matter if we caught any fish or not. We usually didn't. What mattered was the adventure we were on together. Dad often went over and beyond what I saw other fathers do with their kids. Since he didn't have a father growing up, I know my father's resolve was to spend as much time with us as possible. What he would do with us I imagine was exactly what he wished his dad would have done with him.

Dad made that boat feel like home. However, it wasn't the boat that was the defining factor of it being home to us; it was Dad himself.

One day while we hosted one of our epic Gibbonses' pool parties, it hit me. I realized that I looked nothing like my dad. As the kids from our church youth group splashed in the pool and flipped off the diving board, I glanced over at my dad, who was working on the hamburgers on the grill. For a moment I just studied him.

I noticed his cool blue eyes and his athletic build, which only seemed to grow stronger with age. His curly dark hair was turning increasingly gray in his late thirties. He would soon be all white. He had these Major League pitcher legs, which he'd developed through years of bodybuilding. Truth was, the Koreans were also known for their large calves. But it felt good that at least my legs looked like my dad's.

Dad was also hairy. Chest, face, arms, legs... He had hair in every place imaginable, and he prided himself on this. He loved to take his oversize whiskers, wrestle us down on to the floor, and then grind his whiskers into our stomachs. We always laughed and cried at the same time while Dad, merciless, roared in delight. Seeing our confused laughing and crying reactions fueled him to tickle us even more.

Looking at him, no one would guess that he was my birth father. I knew that was part of why people always gawked at our mixed-race family. It was especially unique back in the '70s. My parents were part of breaking barriers that way, though it wasn't a political thing to them, but a marriage that was born out of love.

After that day at the pool, I couldn't help but wonder if my dad was my birth father. I started noticing more differences between myself and my dad. I looked more like Chong than my brother, Doug, who had more of our dad's features.

Why do we look so different?

My parents had always wanted me and my brother not to feel different in any way. Mom would buy us the exact same outfits and toys. Just different colors or slight variances in design that she knew we wouldn't contest or challenge. They always tried to make us fit in.

But I couldn't seem to stop wrestling with my identity and my parents' past.

Maybe I'm not half-white and half-Korean like I've always believed.

Maybe I'm 100 percent Korean.

With this question in my mind, I approached my dad one day. With fear and timidity, I eked out the question.

"Am I Korean or American?" I asked. By American, I assumed he understood that I meant white—his birth son.

His alarmed expression made it clear that he didn't understand how I could even ask such a thing.

"Dave, you're American," he said adamantly.

I could see by his face that he was offended that I had even asked. I believed him. It is scientifically feasible to be genetically from two vastly different races but carry the physical ethnic characteristics of only one.

I wondered about my ethnic heritage, but one thing I never worried about was about to unravel.

CHAPTER SEVEN

Lost in Translation

Police cars parked outside my house. Police officers standing next to my father's car. I was sixteen at the time, coming home from school. My father's new yellow-and-white Chevy Blazer was in its usual place outside in the driveway. The roof was a white hardshell top that you could take off to go four-wheeling or cruising around. This was the most recent car Mom had purchased for my dad.

What the heck is going on?

As I tentatively walked up the cement driveway, I noticed neighbors peering out of their windows. Curious eyes assessing what was happening. Surveying a place that had been violated, I felt like the first responder to a disaster scene. Policemen sat in their patrol cars, while others stood nearby the car. They weren't sure who I was but let me pass by anyway.

When I reached the Chevy, I was startled to see my mom in the backseat. She was weeping behind closed windows. Mascara running down her cheeks. She had a kitchen knife in her hand and was cutting into the seats. I soon learned she'd locked herself in.

It took her a moment before she looked up and saw me. For a moment we locked eyes. Her look of terror is seared into my memory. It reminds me of the famous black-and-white photograph of the naked girl in Vietnam uncontrollably crying as she ran down a street in her war-ravaged city. The same expression of shock and horror stared at me in our driveway. Mom looked like a person that I had never met before.

"Ma'am, please come out of the vehicle," one of the police officers said to my mom. They had been trying to coax her out of the car, but she wouldn't budge. No way was she going to unlock the doors.

I couldn't say anything to her; I was in a state of shock. I had never seen Mom acting this way. I looked for my brother and sister but they weren't home. I started asking the policemen what was happening, but nobody would respond to me. There was only silence, the kind of silence you hear when there is no conceivable answer. A moment when no one knows what to say and you simply feel the pity they have for you. *I'm sorry but your parents need to explain this one to you.* So I just wandered around the driveway in a daze, the way I imagine someone reacts when coming upon a crime scene for the first time. All the while my mom refused to leave the car, sitting inside it, not moving, weeping, and in complete anguish.

The police must have called my dad, because he eventually arrived with his lawyer. Dad was dressed for work, in a tie but no jacket because of the Arizona heat. When he appeared, Dad seemed uneasy. He pulled out a packet of cigarettes and lit one up. He usually tried to hide the fact that he was still smoking cigarettes, because it was not what good Christians did, but today he didn't care. The eyes that always looked steady now nervously shifted back and forth. His movements seemed awkward, quick, and random, like someone trying to calm their nerves. He walked briskly by the Chevy, smoking and talking with his lawyer and not looking at Mom. It was odd—he barely even glanced at her. He didn't act like her husband. He looked lost. Then he saw me. He didn't say anything to me. He couldn't look at me. It was weird how he was avoiding me, not even comforting me.

His silence only added to the nightmare that was unfolding before me.

My mom loved Dad. She loved showering him with clothes, cars, and jewelry. I had never seen them disconnected in any way. I never even saw them fight. Never heard any raised voices or slammed doors. Never even spotted any cynical or frustrated looks. So surely this couldn't be an issue with them. But I just couldn't understand why Mom was weeping uncontrollably and Dad was just standing there, nervously watching her unravel. Why wasn't he doing anything? And who was this lawyer standing nearby him?

Until our City Church pastor arrived, we saw no movement from Mom. It felt comforting when Pastor Simpson arrived. In addition to his large, looming figure, he had a prominent, square jawline, a face that was proportionate to his big frame, and short, thin, wavy brown hair slicked back and parted nicely on the side. It was strange not to see him wearing the suit that we saw him in every Sunday; instead, he wore a pressed light-colored shirt and slacks. When he arrived, you could feel the authority he carried. His physical presence alone demanded respect and brought a sense of calm to everyone's nervousness. He was a looming presence of stability. He greeted the officers, and then went directly to the Chevy Blazer.

As he looked into the vehicle, his face demonstrated great empathy and concern for Mom. He gently and compassionately spoke to Mom:

"Debbie, it's okay. Come on out."

Pastor Simpson knew Mom not by her Korean name, Son Chae, but as Debbie. He knew her, like most at the church did, as Gary's friendly Korean wife.

Mom didn't have to hear him or understand what he was saying. She could tell he cared just by looking into his sympathetic eyes.

This was the man who represented God to her and to our family. We had seen him speak hundreds of times and now were part of the group of insiders in his church. Dad and Mom were leading the college department at City Church. But oddly, Dad didn't speak to the pastor when he arrived, nor did he give him a formal greeting, which my dad had trained us to do as kids. We were trained to look people in the eye, referring to them as "sir" or "ma'am."

Mom opened the door slowly, then climbed out and collapsed into Pastor Simpson's arms. Her body looked frail and weak, literally broken. She cried, her face grimacing like she'd been hit. Yet there were no outward signs of abuse. This was some type of deep, emotional trauma, a kind my sixteen-year-old self couldn't comprehend at this moment.

With his arm around her shoulder, Pastor Simpson began to guide Mom's limp body toward the house. As they started to pass me while I stood inside the garage, I couldn't help speaking.

"Mom, what happened? What's going on?"

She lifted her head up, her eyes swollen from the tears she'd been shedding.

"Your dad had an affair."

Immediately, without thinking, I responded, "Dad would never do that!"

"I hired a detective. I know he did."

I shook my head. Not my dad. Not the best father I knew. The man was my hero. He had valiantly lifted my mom from her poverty in Seoul and made us a home in Maryland. Then he'd led our family out of the tragedy of our house fire in Maryland and garnered the resources and resolve to transport us to Arizona for a fresh start. The dad I knew never fought with Mom; he fought *for* her. He was funny, and loved by all who were important to us. A leader in our new church family. He was the embodiment of the American dream to us. Our hero. This moment and how Mom and Dad were acting made no sense to me.

It's impossible.

Dad didn't say a word to Mom as Pastor Simpson led her up through the garage into the house. All he did was nervously take more drags of his cigarette. He never smoked publicly around us or especially in front of other church members. When the door shut, I looked at my dad, hoping he would allay my fears. I was now in a state of shock.

"Dad, Mom said you had an affair."

He took another drag of his cigarette, looked away, and then looked back at me. It was odd seeing Dad look so nervous. He usually was very calm and confident. I could tell he, too, was overwhelmed.

"She doesn't know what she's talking about," he resolutely said. "It's not true."

His voice sounded different, defeated. His replies were short and to the point. The empathy I had always seen growing up was no longer there. He needed consoling, too, yet there was no conversation with Pastor Simpson, whom he was friends with and had respect for. Instead, my dad spoke only with his lawyer.

For a moment, everything stopped. In the middle of all the chaos unfolding around us, with the police officers still outside by their cars and the gaping rips in the Chevy seats, I replayed the words my dad had spoken to me, yet I couldn't appropriately process them.

I wanted to believe him. But did that mean Mom was lying? Why would she lie about something like that? She mentioned she'd hired a detective. Maybe the detective had made a mistake. Mom must have gotten some inexpensive, inexperienced young amateur detective from some ad in the free "newspaper" they dropped in our driveway every week. My parents loved each other. After everything my mom had been through in Korea, my dad would never cheat on her.

I wanted to believe this so hard, I convinced myself Mom must have been mistaken or at the very least had misunderstood. Something had got lost in translation.

Dad was the foundation of our home. It had never once crossed my mind that Dad would ever betray Mom, and in betraying Mom, betray us. We knew him as a strong Christian leader modeling how to follow Jesus for us. Dad couldn't have had an affair. He had too much to lose: Mom, us, his community, his relationships at church, and his reputation.

That night, a house usually filled with laughter was eerily quiet. Dad left us to spend the night somewhere else. Even though his crisis was with Mom, it felt like he was rejecting all of us children as well. Mom disappeared into the night, too. This would be the first of many trips to the local bars. Seeking to numb her pain, she turned to the very thing that drove her away from her father and her first partner, Chong's birth father. There was no family meeting. No explanation with all of us together. Chong, Doug, and I were just left there alone in the uncertainty of our future. All of us retreated to our bedrooms, where we sobbed. The sound of our weeping behind closed doors still evokes a depth of emotion in me. Sudden tragedy feels like a nightmare you can't wake up from. You don't know if it's real or a bad dream.

I thought my parents had the American dream locked in.

In the haven of my bedroom, I looked at the mementoes of my life. My worn baseball glove by the closet reminded me of the hours Dad had spent playing with us kids. Dad had loved us well. This was during a time when it wasn't necessarily popular for dads to be involved in their children's lives. Dad had endured many wayward balls as he was teaching Doug and me how to become baseball pitchers, like he had been. We'd wildly hurl the baseball and it would bounce off the ground and bruise his legs. If we threw the baseball too high when he caught for us, the ball would literally ricochet against the concrete brick behind him and then inevitably hit his head. Our throwing was so consistently bad that at some point Dad, exasperated, would say, "That's it!" He was done. Irritated, he would quickly walk inside the house. But that only meant he was done for the day. He always felt bad for getting upset, so he would catch for us again the next day.

Dad had been injured and dinged so many times by us, yet he never quit on us. His intensive coaching was so on point that Doug and I made the Little League All Star teams.

So why are you quitting on us now?

It felt like the bedrock of our home had vanished. What remained was a human sinkhole. Nothing about the whole spectacle with Mom in the Chevy, the police cars, and the neighbors peering out the windows at our family seemed real. But when the next morning came, nothing had changed. The house was silent. Dad and Mom were noticeably not present. It was all too real.

Once Mom sobered up, she weighed her options. She pleaded with Dad to come back home. If she was in Korea, she would have literally gotten on her knees and started rubbing her hands together, begging my dad not to leave. She was willing to let go of his affair with this new woman.

However, in our Christian church community, Dad was considered someone who needed to repent. Adultery was a scarlet letter, a clear sign that you weren't right with God. In fact, the church leadership, hearing about his affair, told me I needed to "separate from my dad, who is in sin and not repenting." There was this idea—argued from Scripture—that if someone is living in sin and they are confronted with it and still don't change, it's our responsibility to separate from them with the hope they come back to God. We would separate from them, cut them off, essentially cancel them, because we loved them. The hope was these offenders would come back to God if we essentially cut them from relationship with us. It was a popular thing many Christians did, even to their children. It was called "tough love." For some reason, even as a child, I thought this seemed odd and bogus, especially as it related to my father. How do you separate yourself from your own father? This wasn't about boundaries but a form of punishment. But like any of the rules that I struggled with as a teenager, I reasoned that these spiritual leaders knew better than me.

We thought it was progress when he did come back. All of us were hopeful that our family was going to make it. We earnestly prayed for reconciliation. We were convinced if there was a God, He wouldn't want our family to split up. And God certainly wouldn't want my mom to return to her suffering. Mom had survived the Korean War, an abusive father, an alcoholic and abusive partner, extreme poverty, immigration to America, and even a fire. If anything would kill Mom, it would be her broken heart.

For a while, we all tried to return to the way things were before. From the outside, things looked the same.

But while Dad was home with us, things weren't the same. Trust had been broken. Repair would take time and work.

One day Dad asked me to wash his car, the same Chevy Blazer that Mom had locked herself in. Life seemed like it was starting to heal itself. Dad had had the seats repaired by that point. "No problemo," I said. Due to my allergies, my brother always mowed the grass, so I was glad to fulfill Dad's request. He always did so much for us, so I wanted to demonstrate to my dad that I was developing into a hard worker and not just that kid who watched television all day long. After filling a plastic bucket with dish soap and a large sponge, I began to brush off the backseat. I couldn't help recalling that day again, but I quickly put it out of my mind. As I looked at the mint-like condition of the car, it was possible to pretend nothing had ever happened. The shine had been restored.

All is good.

After washing the exterior, I got out the large industrial vacuum to clean the rugs and the mats. As I lifted the mat on the driver's side, I found a white envelope underneath. Out of curiosity, I opened the envelope and pulled out a thick, nicely designed card. As I read it, I realized it wasn't from Mom or one of his friends.

Two words jumped from the page: *Love, Carolyn.*

My mom's American name was Debbie.

This was the woman Mom had talked about, the woman Dad had denied existed.

I quietly slid the card back into the envelope and finished up the last details of the wash. I slowly made my way back into my bedroom, my only retreat from the craziness unfolding in our family. Barely able to stand, I lay down in bed and wept, realizing Mom had been right all along. I kept repeating to myself:

How could my own father lie to me?

This unspoken thought began to grow in the darkness of my heart. I had no idea how it would soon become relentless in suffocating my inner thoughts. I could feel the negative emotion of my father's betrayal grow in intensity inside me. Once again, my mind jumped to the idea that for a short-term sexual liaison and the attention of some woman he really didn't know, he'd throw my mom and us under the bus.

I didn't know how to handle this conflict inside of me. I never saw conflict resolution modeled. I just did what I always did: I buried his acts of injustice beneath the surface. If someone hurt me, my go-to response was the silent treatment, to become passive-aggressive. Since I was a kid, if I didn't like what my parents asked me to do or if they offended me in some way, I simply refused to talk to them. I'd brood in my room for days, giving the silent treatment to whoever I was upset with.

I didn't know how else to respond but to close the door to my father. It was a primal, instinctive thing to do to protect myself. He had lied to me, so I pushed him away.

After a couple of months, Dad stopped trying to work things out with Mom. He had enough. He once again started living somewhere else. Only my brother would visit him regularly. Doug and my father drew closer together during this time. In fact, Doug ended up becoming my dad's best friend. I'm sure Doug struggled with staying close to both Dad and also to Mom, but for me, it was an easy choice. Dad's relationship with Mom was finished, and I decided to be done with him, too. He couldn't be trusted. All the good days with him prior to the Chevy days were forgotten.

Eventually, my dad had enough of my silence. He came to the house, where he was now a visitor. Dad looked at me with now aging eyes that had lost their glint. His wrinkles and the bags underneath his eyes were becoming more pronounced. He asked:

"Can I talk to you?"

Begrudgingly, I said, "Sure."

After sitting down on the couch in the living room, he turned to me and asked, "Dave, why aren't you talking to me?"

My eyes scanned the carpet below me; I still had a hard time looking at him. I glanced at him and then looked back down to the ground.

"You should know," I tersely replied. "Isn't it obvious?"

As I looked back at him, his expression told me he really didn't know. Deep down I wanted him to confess what he had done, that he had lied to me, that yes, he did have an affair.

Come clean. Keep it real with me. I'm your son.

"Dave, I really don't know."

His sincerity only frustrated me more. He was eager to know why I was keeping a distance from him. I couldn't believe he didn't know. So, exasperated, I responded:

"Well, you remember the time you asked me to wash your Chevy Blazer? When I was cleaning under the driver's side mat, there was an envelope. I opened up the card and saw the words 'Love, Carolyn.'"

For several moments—an eternity inside me—a long pause hung between us.

Just say it. Own up to it.

My heart wanted him to apologize, to admit his wrongdoing and to break up with this woman he was having an affair with. To come back to Mom and all of us. To be a family under one roof again like we were in Maryland. *Just own your wrong and let's move on.*

I wanted him to be the dad I knew growing up.

He took a deep breath.

"Well, everybody makes mistakes."

"That's not good enough," I said tersely with complete disgust as I stood up and walked away.

I'm done with you.

I was convinced that this was a man who cared more about himself than his family. How could he act so irresponsibly? He wasn't safe to me anymore. All the values he had spent years to instill in me now meant nothing. His God, his beliefs, his authority he had in my life—I could care less about them.

The whole Christianity thing became a farce. The leading example of a Christian was my father. Just as our home had collapsed, so did my faith. My faith in God and my faith in my dad.

And my mom? The pain I saw in her was so great that it looked like a thousand souls all at once crying out in anguish. Mom's cries were not just those of one woman in her forties but the cries of a child with an alcoholic father and the grief of a young mom on the run, leaving an abusive partner and suddenly alone again. The demons from the past were crying out from her. It was a pain that went beyond my mom. Her despair sounded like the sorrow that came from generations of suffering. As Mom continued wailing, you could hear the cries of her siblings, her mom, her grandparents, and even the nation of Korea in her broken voice.

CHAPTER EIGHT

한 Han—
a Collective Pain

Han is a concept that is deeply rooted in Koreans. It's a complex array of emotions that deal with sorrow, injustice, resentment, hatred, and anger. Koreans have battled oppression and slavery from Japanese occupation, American imperialism, war, and other atrocities. Many of these memories are still fresh and embedded in the psyche and fabric of Korean culture.

Like the word "jeong," I didn't know this word, "han," even existed till later in life. But I know han was embedded in every cell of my mom's body.

In the weeks and months following the discovery of my dad's affair, my mom still tried to win him back multiple times. She lost respect for herself and it felt like she was begging my father to return.

Mom bought him things to try to woo him back. She would literally do anything possible to get him to come home.

At one point she had even tried to plead with my dad's lover. Mom had little fear now. She found Carolyn's phone number, called her, and started yelling at her.

"Don't you know he's married and has three kids?" She yelled a few choice Korean profanities that Carolyn was clueless about.

Carolyn hung up on her, probably shocked that my mom would dare call her.

Mom had started to drink the moment Dad left her, but once she realized he wasn't coming back to her, her drinking got heavier. We'd never seen Mom drink alcohol before, so it was hard getting used to what seemed to now be a daily habit. As her nights out became more frequent, she would come home drunk in the early morning hours, sometimes brought home by men or acquaintances I'd never seen before. Mom had gone through so much. After all the abuse she had suffered as a child and at the hands of alcoholics, she was becoming one.

In the early morning, I was awakened by someone wailing outside my bedroom window, which was near our front door. It was Mom. I knew that Chong or Doug didn't want to bring her in. They were acting like they were asleep, or maybe they truly were soundly asleep. We were hardly talking to one another, just surviving. I still was hoping one of them would bring Mom inside. After waiting for one of them to answer the door, I finally knew I had to be the responsible one. I was the oldest son. I opened my bedroom door, walked down the hallway, made a right into the living room, and unlocked the front door.

I opened the door and found my mom curled into the fetal position behind a small brick wall that partially hid her from the street. Her mascara was smeared on her face, and the smell of alcohol alerted me to another night at the bar. I found her uncontrollably weeping. Any attempt at consolation was of little help.

I immediately pulled her from the cold cement entryway and lifted her up so she could get her legs under her. As we moved into the living room, we tumbled onto the floor together. With one arm around Mom, I used my other arm to close the door so we wouldn't wake our neighbors. I was leaning against the large front window of the house, my mom now cradled in my arms. I suddenly felt like the parent comforting a child.

Shaking and crying, she kept repeating herself in a deep, mournful wailing, like you hear at a funeral in Korea, "Why me? Why me? Why me?" Then her eyes turned downward and her tears kept flowing. Then she kept repeating, "Why? Why? Why?"

The old smell of alcohol became stronger.

"The only reason I'm alive is for you kids."

Mom's face was one of excruciating pain. She was lost.

Her accent sounded thicker, her words harder to decipher.

"You're the man of the house now," she declared.

I didn't respond; she wouldn't have remembered what I said even if I did say something. Everything in me resisted. This was supposed to be the time of my life: playing sports, dating, partying, and experimenting with new teenage freedoms.

Mom curled up into a ball on the multicolored green shag carpet in our living room. She barely resembled the mom I knew. During this tumultuous season, Mom had aged overnight. Her makeup got heavier. Some nights she wouldn't come home at all; other times she arrived with glazed eyes and the effects of alcohol evident in her demeanor. Sometimes she'd be laughing, would wobble in to look at us, then greet us with a cheery, drunk voice before going to her room. Her smile was crooked and forced. But other nights, like this one, she came home overwhelmed with grief. Her eyes looked lost in hopelessness. The kind of eyes you see when someone is in shock and locked in a never-ending nightmare.

I'm not ready to assume my dad's responsibility.

After holding her for a while, I helped Mom up once again and guided her back to her room. The king-size bed seemed to swallow her petite body. It seemed even more depressing that Dad wasn't in that bed. I closed the door of her bedroom.

I went back to my bedroom with memories of my worst nightmares.

Since I was a child, I'd had night terrors of my parents dying, of their physical lives being suddenly taken away. But this type of dying was something I'd never even thought about. Physically alive, but mentally, emotionally, and spiritually dead. Mom's drinking was spiraling out of control. Ulcers and sicknesses were more frequent. Her physical body started to turn on itself.

Mom's energetic spirit and her contagious laughter were a distant memory.

The divorce proceeding was to take place in Phoenix. I told my sister I'd take Mom to the courtroom. It was the last thing I wanted to do, but I felt it was the elder son's responsibility. Chong had still been picking up the pieces of responsibility left to her by our dad and mom. Doug was too young and still finding it hard to deal with the separation of the parents he loved. He was doing his best as a young teenager. I felt the most compassion for my brother because he was quieter and more reserved. It was challenging for all of us to share our feelings, but it must have been even more difficult for him.

As Mom and I walked down the shiny, waxed floor of the courtroom, I was struck that this environment seemed so formal, sterile, and clinical. Yet it was here that people were dealing with some of the most dramatic human conflicts. Entering the courtroom, I saw places for the interested parties and family to formally settle in; I took a seat far from the wooden wall that separated the audience from the main participants of the proceedings. I couldn't help thinking that the judge's seat looked like a towering wooden throne with the American flag and the Arizona flag prominently displayed behind it. In front of the judge's bench, to his right, was where Mom would uncomfortably sit behind a wooden table with her lawyer. I can't imagine how out of place she must have felt as an immigrant, more culturally Korean than American. Dad entered the room and sat on his side with his lawyer. As a stenographer, Dad had worked in these very rooms for years. I knew the discomfort Mom felt about being there, but these were familiar stomping grounds for my dad. Even Dad's lawyer was someone he had worked with before and was also a personal friend.

As comfortable as he might have felt, my dad never looked me in the eye the whole time I was inside the courtroom. His eyes were fixed on the judge or his lawyer.

Then there was Mom, with her broken English. Alone with some unfamiliar lawyer. The only person she knew in that room besides me was my dad. She knew the proceedings were meant to be quick and uneventful, but she couldn't hold back the tears. The finality of the moment overwhelmed her. The forensic language and the participants were all unrecognizable. When the judge started reading the dissolution of the marriage, I could tell that Mom didn't seem to know what was being said anymore. Her eyes darted back and forth, trying to comprehend the moment. Eventually she locked her gaze on my father as if he were the only one in the room. As the judge and lawyers kept deliberating, Mom began pleading with my father, crying out, her voice trembling like it probably had when she'd felt alone as a child in her hometown in Korea.

Mom couldn't contain herself anymore. She blurted out: "Gary, I don't want this divorce. I don't want this divorce."

Mom's face was filled with anguish, her eyes damp and red. She just looked over at my father in desperation. Her lawyer vainly attempted to comfort her.

When I heard my mom crying and begging my father not to proceed with the divorce, I ran out of the courtroom, not wanting anyone to see my tears. Mom didn't need to share my pain. She had enough to deal with. Generations of suffering were her inheritance. I stood in the long glossy corridor waiting for everything to be over. This was now my default way of dealing with things. Just run away. Ignore the drama. Even if I'd been aware of the pattern back then, I don't think there was anything I could have done about it. The pain felt too overwhelming. I felt like I was drowning in Mom's suffering and injustice.

After the proceedings, Mom came out. We walked together to the car. Not a word was spoken as I drove her home. We remained in a painful silence. Mom had a dazed look on her face. She was still in a state of shock.

Their split was now public and official. Reconciliation was no longer an option. All the prayers for them to come back together again seemed like wasted effort. With Dad now officially divorced from Mom, we all felt he'd made his choice. Not only with Mom, but also with us. He would no longer have any authority in my life. No respect, for sure.

And the Christian thing Dad had led us into...I was done with it. As for God, I struggled with His existence. If He was real, why would He permit such suffering?

CHAPTER NINE

Alone

The first thing I noticed was their height. Some of the guys had long, black cascading hair glimmering in the summer sun. They had that relaxed Island vibe and their ominous size was something to take seriously. On a field in the neighborhood next to ours, a group of jacked high school guys played tackle football, and after seeing me, they asked me to join. This was new. I didn't remember such openness to me from public school kids before. And this was the cool, athletic, jock group. I couldn't resist. None of them knew the awkward middle schooler I used to be. He was long gone. I had little regard for my life now and I was open, even eagerly looking to take risks.

As a teenager, my baby fat was finally starting to get redistributed to other portions of my growing body. I began lifting weights. I started to comb my hair and use product. I cared about my fashion.

Mom had always been the one who made sure we were looking good, but now I was taking on that responsibility. My dad had bought me a motorcycle before all the turmoil went down in our family. I enjoyed riding the Arizona streets in shorts and no shirt. I was proudly and uncomfortably showing off my slowly maturing athletic physique.

As we picked teams, I noticed the teenagers that surrounded me. A couple of them were Asian—large Samoan-looking behemoths. Their bodies proudly carried a collection of scars on their faces, arms, and legs from other teams they had played against. The shirts and pants they wore looked sweaty and roughed up.

"Have you played much?" one of the guys asked me.

"Yeah, some," I said.

Some meant hardly any. When I was younger, my dad had enrolled me in a tackle football program for kids. I barely played. My red-and-white uniform always remained spotless after each game. I was afraid to hit people and injure myself, even though we were wearing helmets and pads. I didn't understand the need to hit people, even with equipment on, with such velocity. It seemed foolish. Dad would come to the games disappointed that I wasn't playing. One time walking away from a game that I didn't play in again, he muttered under his breath that our efforts "were a waste of time."

Things were different now.

From the moment the opposing team hiked the ball, I played with reckless abandon. I chased after the quarterback, attempting to either sack him or get him to throw the ball away. I pounded into players, pushing them back, or barreled into them with overzealous intensity. After a series of plays like this, I noticed one of the guys who was larger than me respectfully gazing at me like, *Bro, who are you? Damn, you're good.* I had hit him hard multiple times with a couple of intense blocks. My rambunctious play was a bit much for a neighborhood pickup game.

My concern for personal injury was gone. I concluded that if I didn't worry about my physical body, I could be dangerous. While these guys were playing casual football, I was zealously pummeling and pushing them with all that I had. I know now I must have been working through all that pent-up anger toward my dad and the powerlessness I felt. And the praises and smiles of the other guys after I made a good play felt gratifying, even comforting.

"Whoa! Hey, what's your name?" this huge Samoan-looking guy asked.

"I'm Dave Gibbons. I'm half-Korean and half-American. I know I look a hundred percent Korean, but yeah—I'm not adopted." I always felt a need to be very specific about my racial identity. My emphasis was always on "American." I wanted them to know that I was one of them.

"Well, bro, you should try out for the Mesa High School football team and play with us. You're good."

This was the starting tackle of the JV (junior varsity) football team telling me this. It was one of the first times I felt such affirmation from a peer who would be considered "cool." It was a good feeling. And Mesa High was one of the large public high schools renowned for their football and wrestling programs.

It was the start of the summer after my parents' divorce. I needed a diversion from all the pain. In that moment, I realized I could play high school football—the all-American ticket to popularity and acceptance in the high school ecosystem. I followed the Samoan guy's advice and did exactly that. I left City Academy and returned to the public school. With my father now gone, he was powerless to keep me at a Christian school. I wanted to forget God, along with anything my father said was good for me, like the church and the Christian school. I wanted no part of it. It was a direct way of disrespecting my father and his desire for me to be a good Christian young man.

After feeling the invisibility that comes with divorce, added to the invisibility of being a legal "alien" in America, I was desperately looking for some tribe to belong to. A place to be seen and known. Football became that home. It was good for me because it was a legal way to physically release my frustrations. Football became a place to vent my adolescent emotional traumas. Violence was accepted on the field, and even applauded. I could hit people without consequences. It was an acceptable place to deal with my emotional wounds, and perhaps prove to my father that I could make it without him by becoming an elite athlete. Without his help, I could find societal acceptance and respect. Being aggressive on the field also made me popular on campus. The coaches that summer treated me like I was this new football prodigy. I was an exciting new starting prospect who had come out of nowhere from some private school nearby.

This would have been exciting for anybody, but this was monumental for a kid who had felt invisible. Because of my determined attitude and ability to play hard, the coaches experimented with putting me in multiple positions. I hadn't played tackle football or any organized sport in middle school. This newfound attention was flattering, but challenging as well. I tried the best I could, but there was a litany of football jargon and plays to learn for someone new to the sport at one of the top high school programs in the state. In the end, I told the coaches I just wanted to keep things simple. I could block on offense or tackle on defense. I wanted them to put me in a position that wouldn't require the level of understanding necessary for a quarterback or another high-skill player. I wanted to focus on something I knew I could do well and not have to think too much on the field. I did not want to risk failing and lose this feeling of being accepted. That risk was too great. I knew if I could play one of the less complex positions, I was a lock to be on the team.

Just turn me loose.

Dad had instilled into me a confidence that I could do anything if

I tried, and he taught me this through our hours of practicing throwing baseballs or footballs at one another in the front yard. I'd say, "I can't do this, Dad." He'd say, "Can't never do nothing." A triple negative. A double negative was improper in English. Dad, being a voracious reader, was a master of the English language. He had a rich vocabulary, which made this triple negative more memorable: "Can't never do nothing."

During the practices, I had fun unleashing who I was—a wild, out-of-touch, misfit Asian kid who had a real chip on his shoulder. I would breathe erratically, like a bull ready to gore my opponents, huffing and puffing on the line like I couldn't wait to hit you. I wanted to be unpredictable and overly intense! Our coaches told us if you hit a player three times in a row as hard as you can, they would give up. They were right. I did this to players much heftier than me and they would succumb. I'm sure they hadn't met an Asian guy like me before. I was the opposite of the stereotype of a weak, deferential Asian. With my success in football, my confidence grew.

At the time, our team had a star running back who would later become an NFL pro football player. He was fast and knew how to run. As an offensive lineman who blocked for him, I loved seeing him jet up the field after we opened a hole for him. Often, we would make not only one block, but sometimes two on a play. One time, we played a team that had this offensive tackle whom I had to go up against, a large mass of muscles who said he was sixteen but looked like he was twenty-five. He was at least one foot taller and wider than me and probably weighed twice my body weight, even though I was big for my size, having beefed up on beer and steak. During one play, I fired off the line like I'd been taught. I would go lower than the other player to get leverage. But this time, even though I'd gone lower, it was like running into a concrete wall. I bounced off this mound of muscles and could only look up at him from the ground while he ran past me like a bull. That didn't stop me from bouncing up and going back for more.

The drive to be accepted by the other athletes—and, of course, the girls—because of my football skills was a great motivation for me.

I played so well because I wasn't afraid of hurting myself. I didn't care about my body. Nothing I felt on the field was as painful as what it was like to be in my own home, wondering where my mom was, or hearing her crying at night when she finally made it back from the bar. My worst fears had already happened when my family blew up.

Besides, I liked playing a sport in which your ethnicity and physical characteristics had little to do with your acceptance on the team. I loved that when we put on our helmets and pads, we all looked alike. The difference would not be our eyes or accents, but how we played the game.

Sports helped me gain confidence, but still the bullying didn't stop. After a challenging practice, we were taking off all our sweat-drenched equipment and throwing it in these large rolling laundry containers. Hanging up our pads in our locker or throwing the smaller pads into a bin. Then making our way to the group shower area, where rows of multiple metal shower heads were neatly and strategically placed on one pole. One by one we entered into the showers, joking around while we got ourselves cleaned up.

I was soaping up when I felt this warm stream of liquid hitting my leg. The starting running back, the one who would later play in the NFL, was urinating on my leg. When I noticed it and looked at him, he just started laughing. The sad thing was that he was Asian, too, of Tongan and Polynesian descent. I came to learn a brutal truth. Just because you look alike doesn't mean you experience the same pain. Sometimes that makes you more inclined to bully, simply to prove you're not like that other guy. The slur of being an "Uncle Tom" became real to me.

Even as his urine ran down my leg, I laughed with the guy, yet I walked out of the locker room feeling humiliated. And later, disgusted with myself that I didn't fight back again. I know the incident might have been just another random immature teenage jock thing, but I had thought my teammates would be different. Football would provide opportunities to earn respect, where my racial identity wouldn't matter, or so I'd thought.

I had trusted football to make me someone who deserved respect. My mantra had been: Outwork people. Hustle will make up for skill. If I failed in football or in life, it wouldn't be because of effort. This was the mantra I owned. I learned one can have a high tolerance for pain. Some call it a learned helplessness, meaning that if you're confronted with a constant state of pain, abuse, or trauma, you get used to it, so much so that when you can avert it, you still choose not to run away from the hurt, because you've gotten so used to it feeling inescapable. I was learning to live with pain but not be overcome by it.

It was slowly becoming clear that the football community wasn't going to be family for me. I was still lost. And alone.

CHAPTER TEN

Rocky Mountain High

H ey, Gibbons. I hear you like playing racquetball."

The gruff voice took me by surprise. I had just arrived home and pulled my motorcycle into the garage. The short and stocky forty-year-old standing on our driveway was our neighbor from four houses down. Dave Bunt and his family had recently moved to our neighborhood, and he had started a position as the new youth pastor at my old church. He and his wife, Stephanie, had a large family, and they were regularly hosting teenagers or kids who had been struggling. Their house resembled Grand Central Station for wayward kids. They were a large family but they still took in other kids who were from broken homes.

He had heard about me from others at the church who said, "Don't waste your time on Dave Gibbons. He's too far gone." I was one of those "worldly" kids whom parents didn't want their children to hang around.

Pastor Bunt heard this as a challenge. It was a confirmation that he needed to spend time with me.

"Want to play some racquetball sometime?" he asked me with a large bright smile. "We can go for a Slurpee at 7-Eleven afterwards."

The racquetball I could pass on, but the Slurpee was hard to say no to. "Sure! Let's do it." I always liked a good challenge, so why not? It'd be fun to beat the old religious guy. Besides, he was a neighbor. Perhaps that wasn't coincidental. Pastor Dave would later play a key role in my life that would mature and direct me in ways I didn't know I needed.

As Bunt walked back down the sidewalk to his house, I watched his swagger. He had greased-back black hair like Elvis and large muscular arms. He was a tradesman. A burly, blue-collar mechanic who knew how to work and put in long hours. He had a small round beer gut, too. Not sure, though, it was from beer, since he was a fundamentalist Christian pastor. When I first met him, I wasn't impressed. Initially, he came across as cocky, even a bit arrogant. I had been to Pastor Bunt's youth meetings a couple of times, and while he was a good speaker and challenged us to learn to communicate, his teaching manner felt a bit too authoritarian. He'd shout at inattentive young people to "Zip the lip!" He'd call you out if you were sleeping while he was speaking. He carried my dad's authority, yet it felt more raw, crass, and direct. Dad could communicate things with a look and no words; Bunt would make sure to use the force of his voice with his stern looks. It was a *Don't test me because you don't want to know what I'll do to you* sort of look.

On this day, though, something was different. The firm and demanding demeanor was gone. In fact, there was a certain humility when he asked if I wanted to play racquetball with him. After Mom's episode in the driveway, Pastor Simpson must have told Pastor Bunt to start spending time with me, because he started popping over to our house more frequently. Originally, I didn't want to hang with him. He didn't seem cool at all with his greased hair. I mean, he was a pastor. I was having too much fun playing football, making new friends. I was done with God stuff for now. I was experimenting with the things City Academy and City Church forbade us to do. But after he discovered that my brother, Doug, and I enjoyed playing competitive racquetball, the youth pastor figured out a way to connect to me.

Over the next few months, he'd come over and ask me to play racquetball again every so often. After repeatedly beating him silly, I started to kind of like him. He was similar to my dad in how he could take getting hit with the balls and keep on going. He constantly got hit on the butt or the back with racquetballs I was zinging toward the front wall. The rubber balls left perfectly round bruises in multiple spots on his body. There was certainly some type of foolish delight in seeing him get hit by my ball. But he kept on playing, donning these large round bruises on his back. Again, like my dad.

One of those nights, after he lost multiple games, I asked him a question. Bunt later told me it was a question no one had ever asked him before and never asked him since. With our rackets in his car trunk and our giant Slurpees in our hands, we sat on the curb, our T-shirts drenched and perspiration dripping from our heads. I still wasn't quite used to the Arizona heat, even at night. It was close to midnight as we enjoyed our frozen drinks and heard the occasional car rolling by in the distance.

Out of nowhere came a question that got unearthed from deep inside my soul.

"How does a person fall out of love?"

My parents' separation still confounded me. Instead of quickly giving me a pat answer or even expressing his own curiosity, Pastor Bunt simply gave me an earnest look, one that seemed to say, *That's a really good question, kid.*

For several moments, we sat in silence.

"Let's go home," he finally said.

He gave the right answer. Silence.

❧

That summer, right around the time I had started tasting some measure of peer acceptance from playing football, Bunt invited me to a Christian youth camp in Telluride, Colorado. Regardless of what the organizers had in mind, I saw this camp as a time to escape from our family troubles, have fun with friends, and par-tay. Though at the last moment we wisely didn't bring alcohol, we were still ready to make a nuisance of ourselves.

The truth was I still struggled to fit in, even with the new set of guys around me. Many of my football teammates had known each other and played together since they were very young. Every day I constantly compared myself to others who were more skilled socially, academically, and athletically. I had found a new identity to cling to, but in reality I still felt like I didn't belong, like I was still a misfit. I could be like them but my physical appearance would always make me stand out, especially in America at this time.

There were lots of misfits heading to camp, kids from my old school and church. Moments after getting on the bus, I saw the biggest one.

There's Jesus.

That's the nickname I gave Matthew Henry to make fun of him. He'd been a friend of mine since elementary school. I recognized him at once, but I avoided him. In his thick black rims and over-size denim pants, Matthew was the prototypical nerd. A part of me knew he wasn't one of the cool kids, but there was another part of me that liked him, that secretly looked up to him. Matthew was part of a group of four guys I had grown up with earlier at the Academy. They were unusually mature for being high schoolers, and Pastor Bunt had begun paying extra attention to them for this reason. They were on the unspoken leadership track.

Back in fourth grade, Matthew and I played together and even stayed at each other's house. His room, dark with the curtains drawn, was like a wizard's den. It was filled with books, lights, and little inventions he was working on. His room was Godric's Hollow in the West Country (home of the Dumbledores and the Potters). Both his parents were smart and loved education. His mom, Mrs. Marilyn Henry, was an anomaly as she rose to leadership at the City Academy and was a principal there for many years. The tall and full-figured woman with brown curly hair and a huge smile was somehow able to endure years of misogynistic attitudes and oppressive hierarchical systems. Many in the church thought a woman shouldn't be a principal or a pastor.

Over the years, I had grown to have a hidden respect for Matthew. He didn't care what others thought of him; he never hesitated in speaking his mind or standing up for what was right. He was like his mom. Despite others' opinions, they kept plugging away doing what they thought was right.

When I was younger, I had a quick, sarcastic tongue, so there were many times I'd be ignorantly laughing with others, yet Matthew wouldn't laugh, especially if it had to do with God. He'd become serious, even upset at our frivolity. He'd perk up with righteous indignation. "This isn't right," he'd say, and walk out of the room either angry or frustrated with our coarse jesting. I secretly liked that about Matthew. He was a teenager of conviction and willing to go against the crowd. He cared only about pleasing One. I liked how he owned who he was however odd it may have seemed to others. He had more purpose and conviction than anybody I knew. I didn't meet too many high school kids with conviction like that who were willing to take ridicule for what they believed. To disregard what others thought about him was unusual among the people I knew, young or old. It was as if he had this unoffendable heart.

I also liked how Matthew prayed. His prayers had serious conviction; he emotionally engaged God like He was real. Again, this was something I hadn't seen in too many high school students. I was astonished by his hunger to learn new things. He learned how to master puppets to entertain children. He tried to sing. He even learned how to play the accordion. He had a willingness to do whatever it took to connect people with his faith and God.

Pastor Bunt, of course, loved Matthew because of his willingness to serve and his ability to play music. He would lead others in songs. He was maximizing every gift he had. He was all in. I saw how it was the mature kids who were attracted to Matthew. They looked past the normal teenage awkwardness and unattractive physical habits he had and saw his heart. I guess I did, too, but of course I didn't say it to him or to anyone else.

Our camp was divided into multiple teams. You got points for being kind, listening to the messages attentively, performing skits, and winning the games they would plan for us. I enjoyed having fun excursions with my friends, but I really loved the camp-wide rugged challenges. Local athletes attending camp were able to showcase their talents and impress their peers, and since I was now a public school football player, I was determined to win. The grueling summer practices had prepared me for these types of games.

One day the camp director of the games announced a new competition.

"The first ones to get to the top of the falls will acquire points for your respective teams."

Everybody felt inspired to race up the mountain, where Bridal Veil Falls soared nearby. The 365-foot waterfall spilled out of the edge of a box canyon high above us. To get up the falls, you had to hike over huge granite and volcanic rocks and boulders scattered throughout the forests filled with Engelmann spruce, Colorado blues, subalpine fir, quaking aspen, cottonwood, and ponderosa pine. Motivated by an opportunity to prove myself to others and to demonstrate my athletic prowess, I put my resolute game face on and I started running up toward the falls.

Initially I was ahead of the pack. By the time I reached the top of Bridal Veil Falls, I could hear the roar of the water falling thirty-three stories down, crashing onto the rock formations, and cascading to a pool and more boulders below. A light mist of water hovered around the falls. As I sucked in air, I looked ahead to see who else might have survived this arduous climb. There was one camper slightly in front of me who was about to win. The only way I could beat this kid would be to jump over the small stream that led to the waterfall only twenty yards away.

You got this, Gibbons. Go for it.

When you're sixteen, you think you can do anything. I took a deep breath, then began running toward the stream. As I launched myself into the air, my jump looked perfectly distanced, but as I hit the other side, my rubber tennis shoes slipped out from under me. I didn't account for how slippery the rocks were. My body slammed down on the rock and soon I found myself chest deep into the stream. I looked down and saw the edge of the waterfall so close, with the current pulling on me fast. I tried pulling myself up but I couldn't move. My legs locked up and my upper body was exhausted from the climb. I tried moving, but I had no energy. I tried again.

I had nothing left.

The Rocky Mountain air was thin; the elevation was over 10,000 feet, so my lungs gasped for oxygen. I knew I was done unless someone helped me. I didn't know how long I could hold on to the rock. All I could envision was my body drifting and then tumbling over the waterfall onto the hard rocks below.

"Help! Help!"

My voice seemed swallowed by the thunderous sound of the falls. Fortunately, the camper I had overtaken was nearby. He quickly pulled me out.

"Thanks, man," I said. As I stood up, clothes and shoes dripping with water, I tried to act nonchalant. "Man, that was a close call."

The other camper didn't know what to say. He seemed to be in shock, having watched me almost go over the cliff. He gave me a half-hearted smile and said, "Yeah, sure." We were both thinking the same thing.

I could have died.

For a few moments, I caught my breath as more kids arrived at the top. My pants and part of my shirt were drenched with water. Soon I saw Pastor Bunt as I was coming down off the mountain. He caught up to me and started walking next to me.

"Heard what happened to you, Dave. You okay?"

I wondered how he had found out so quickly. I gathered my composure and told him I was fine. He leaned in and looked at me with his big, dark eyes.

"Do you think God is trying to tell you something?"

I laughed. "Nah, I don't think so. See you."

With half my body still dripping with water from being in the stream, I began heading back down the mountain. I didn't want anybody thinking I was scared. And I didn't want him to believe that I was thinking about God.

By this time in my life, I had developed an externally tough skin. After being called all kinds of names—a Chinaman, Chink, Kink, Slant Eyes—I had resolved not to let others see how their words affected me. I had chosen to stop physically fighting others but instead to demonstrate excellence by my actions. I had adopted a more relentless attitude. I knew I might not be the most talented person out there, but I had a quiet resolve that would never quit. If I showed up, I'd be all in. That inner fortitude came from my mom. She could handle abuse, poverty, war, ridicule, shame, death, and then immigrating to a new land, learning the language, and raising a family. I asked myself, *What challenge do I have that is as tough as hers?*

However, I did have another type of resolve.

God didn't make sense to me anymore.

I blamed God for my parents' divorce. He couldn't be real if He allowed such painful tragedies to occur. Didn't God know how much my mom had already suffered in life? Why wouldn't He prevent something that would wreck a family?

I would later hear that God gives us the freedom to make choices. This freedom is gifted to us because He loves us, but the choices we make are ours. I might have wanted to blame God for what my dad did, but God didn't force my dad to do anything. When Pastor Bunt asked me whether God was trying to tell me something, I was internally thinking *maybe*. I wasn't ready to confront a relationship with God. To me, He still could have prevented the pain my family suffered.

I now know, even in my limited understanding, that God can speak to people in many ways. While we often look for God through some spectacular event, God has also spoken to people tenderly. This gentle aspect of God became more attractive to me.

⌒

"What is your purpose?"

The question from the well-groomed gray-haired man at basecamp in Colorado came near the end of his message about Daniel. That night's special speaker at camp was Bud Bierman, a professor at

Bob Jones University in South Carolina, who was respected by many of the kids in our church. He described Daniel being thrown into the lions' den for refusing to worship other gods and God saving his life. Eventually Daniel went on to become a wise government official in Babylon, rising to become a trusted leader even though he was an outsider as a Jew.

Bud wasn't overly charismatic delivering the message, and he wasn't dramatically different than any of the other preachers I had heard in my life. His tone was gentle. Modulation even. He didn't seem like the normal evangelist type. I don't remember anything he said about Daniel except for one line:

"Daniel had a purpose in life."

As I was sitting in the back row, goofing off with my friends, inwardly that phrase kept echoing in my mind. *Daniel had a purpose.* I wondered what was happening to me. I started feeling like I was the only person in the room.

What is my purpose?

That question kept echoing relentlessly inside me.

My mom and dad's purpose was to have a successful life—as measured by what we had materially—and then in seeing us succeed. But once they had the dream, it didn't seem fulfilling. Then everything fell apart.

Something inside me began to quake. Thoughts and questions along with anger and regret about my parents' divorce surfaced once again. For a moment I saw the fallacy of the life I had tried to create for myself. I had built walls to protect my fragile sense of identity while trying to be in the same room as the cool kids. But I had lost something so precious to my younger self: my curiosity, my wonder, and the ability to be okay with mystery. As a young child, I explored the world with an openness and positive expectancy. But now I found myself focused on proving to others that I was some force to be reckoned with. My vision of the world became small, inward, and myopic.

An invitation was given to the audience to give your life to God. Even though I had heard these invitations hundreds of times in church and at the academy, this time seemed different. Why would this walk up the aisle be different? Where before there was fear associated with the invitation, this time it was more about me seeking a reality.

Is God really real?

I knew that if God was as powerful as others said, then my guess was I could use the help. And if He is that powerful, why wouldn't I surrender everything to Him, especially if He is for me and not against me? I felt I had nothing to lose to give God one more shot.

That first step from the back row into the main aisle was the hardest. It seemed like a boulder was anchored to my right foot. As I made my way to the front, I could see the heads turning and the faces staring in disbelief that the rebellious kid was coming to Jesus. Even Pastor Bunt appeared shocked, his eyes wide open in disbelief, as I was walking toward him. By the time I reached him, he could see I was unusually sober and serious. He grabbed my hand and shook it, bringing me closer to him and bending his head toward my ear.

"Why are you coming forward?" he asked while someone was playing the piano in the background.

I thought of my fourth grade friend and how it seemed like he had a real purpose in his life.

"Listen, if God can become real to me like He is to Matthew Henry, I'll do anything."

Pastor Dave appeared surprised that I had mentioned Matthew as someone I respected.

This camp had been a reminder to me that there was something unique about Matthew. The weird guy, the contrarian, the misfit. By now I had trouble seeing anybody as authentic, but Matthew was the real deal. He had the courage to be himself.

With a smile and a surprised expression on his face, Pastor Dave added, "Well, you need to read the Bible. That's how God speaks to us today. Would you like someone to help you?"

I shook my head. "No. If God's real, He doesn't need anyone's help."

I wasn't trying to challenge God; it was more that my heart was curious.

If God is real, then this will be nothing for Him.

In the morning, I woke up feeling the same way I had the night before. Wanting to escape from everyone else, I walked outside the main campgrounds into a wide-open field where the tall grass had turned mostly golden brown. The fresh smell of pine and aspen filled my senses. I sneezed a couple times because I was allergic to the evergreen pollen floating in the air. All around the slightly sloped landscape stood trees soaring to the skies. Nearby, the majestic Rocky Mountains encircled me. The blue sky was dotted with clouds. In the middle of the field sat a massive granite rock that seemed to be calling my name. So I went over and sat on it and looked up to the heavens.

"God, if you're real, I need you to connect to me today. Otherwise, I'm chucking this Christianity thing." It sounded a bit disrespectful but I was earnest in my request.

As I opened up the Bible, I read words I had heard before but never fully understood. For years I had listened to preachers who appeared like they had all the answers, yet I sat there before God still full of questions. Full of pain. Full of doubt.

How could I know Him, and know that I know Him?

How could I be sure that He's real?

How could this connection—this experience and relationship—be authentic and true, like any other relationship?

That was what I longed to know the most. I was searching for love again. The parents I thought were in love weren't anymore. And at the same time, the loveless life of my mom was destroying her.

That day, on that rock in Telluride, I felt a presence of the supernatural. Some would call it an energy. A life force. A higher power. A Spirit. It was God to me. Jesus.

I must have stayed there a few hours. It seemed like minutes. But every one of my questions that I had were answered. I didn't know exactly what my future would look like, but I felt someone would be there to hold me. I felt I was given a promise. That there would be one that would never leave me. He would be my Guide. He would be my Father in any way I needed. He was inviting me to an adventure. He wanted to show me what I thought I'd lost and more. He wanted to take me beyond the small world I was living in.

That day I felt like God met me. He promised He would be a Father to the fatherless. I would need this understanding for what was coming. I felt like a child again with my eyes wide open.

CHAPTER ELEVEN

Twenty-Five Seconds

Neuroscientists say in twenty-five seconds of concentrated meditation you can create a new neuropathway, a highway that your neurons track, a new way of thinking. We all have narratives that form a mind-set or a pattern of thinking. This mind-set moves us toward how we choose to live. At the start of my senior year, I decided to adopt a new mind-set. Is it possible that I can do anything with God's help? I started to believe that I could.

Things had changed for me after going to camp. I had changed. Mom noticed this as well. I would learn later in life that after my Telluride experience, unbeknownst to me, Mom called her best friend to talk about me:

"Okcha, something happened to my son, Dabid. He's different. He listens to me now. He bought me flowers. He's a good boy. Something happened to him. He's changed."

Despite the changes, my aspiration was still to play football at the public high school with the ambitious hope of earning a college scholarship. After enduring the hellish, two-a-day summer practices in 100 degree temperatures, I had survived to make the first string team. Those aspirations changed after a practice when the coaches called me into the football office near the locker rooms. As I sat inside the spartan office, I noticed the family photos in their frames on the desk, then I saw a picture of our coach from his college football days.

"Sit down, Dave," the head coach said.

Concern was etched on his face. The head coach was clean-cut and had an athletic build and was a graduate from BYU (Brigham Young University). His face was gentle, and he had a ruddy complexion. He resembled many of the football players who I found were the meanest, baddest guys on the field, yet were completely the opposite off it. Gentle, kind, and artistic. Next to our head coach stood Coach Zimmerman, the heir apparent. Coach Zimmerman was the one who had spent the most time guiding me to be the best I could be. He wore round wired spectacles that highlighted his bright observant eyes. Everybody knew he was an assistant coach on the rise—energetic, eyes lit, hustling, constantly pumping us up if we did something right, and getting on us if we didn't.

The head coach smiled at me and went straight to the point. Zimmerman nervously rubbed his chin, looking at me, knowing the news was not going to be good. He knew what was coming.

"Dave, I'm sorry but the Arizona Interscholastic Association declared you ineligible to play this year. I'm really sorry. Our hands are tied. There's nothing we can do about it."

He was right. Because local high schools had been recruiting other players from other high schools, the state had recently ruled that transfer students couldn't play for their first year at the new school. This was meant to curtail the transferring of star athletes, which they considered unfair. My dad was irritated and thought it was "ridiculous." We filed a challenge to the Arizona Interscholastic Association, but ultimately lost the appeal for me to play in this crucial year when college scouts came to watch.

Even though my dad hadn't shown up for many of my activities after my parents' separation, he made it out to the appeal hearing. It was something I didn't expect him to be so persistent about. I saw his disgust and disappointment after he heard the verdict. I knew my dad appreciated sports. It was probably a long shot, but maybe he had that glimmer of hope that Doug or I could go pro someday. I was dreaming my football accomplishments would make him proud of me. If I got a college scholarship, I might potentially have a shot at the NFL. But now that option was gone, too. There didn't seem much common ground my dad and I could build upon. Regardless, it felt good to have my dad fight for me. I didn't say much to him about his efforts but his determined engagement in this process felt good. This was the dad I remembered from before the day my mom locked herself up in the car.

I took this closed door as a sign for me to go back to the City Academy to focus on God. If I was meant to be the first Asian player in the NFL, it would have happened. I had conviction that if I couldn't control it, then I would accept it for the good. Things would turn out better somehow. Instead of being overly dark and negative, I chose to be hopeful. I had this feeling that winter could be long, but spring could come in one day. It must have been the genetic optimism my mom had possessed no matter what hardship she was facing. It was about managing mystery, perhaps even embracing it.

Mom once owned this kind of optimism, but it was now long gone. She was still struggling with life without Dad.

Mom once had a dream for her future, and she thought she found it when she met my dad. But now, almost two decades after they married, she was living a very different vision of life. Even as her small body continued to age, she regularly would remain standing for ten to twelve hours every day, working five and sometimes even six days a week. Her positive energy at work never ceased while she cut and styled hair at a boutique salon in Tempe, Arizona. To make sure her skills and techniques were up to date, she would frequently travel to New York City. She quickly learned and was highly adaptive. Mom brought a colorful energy to any room she entered. She appeared strong to anyone who saw her outside our home. Yet if you saw her in her favorite bright red shorts at home, you'd notice her many blue varicose veins scattered throughout her legs, from her ankles to her thighs. Evidence of the blood backing up in her veins from standing all day long. Mom had worked hard all her life but never complained about it.

Mom's focus turned to us. We were the reasons she chose to keep living.

"You should be a dentist," she told me one day.

It was a common thing for immigrant Asian parents to want you to become either a doctor or a lawyer, but at the time I thought it was such a random suggestion.

"The last thing I want to do is to be digging into people's mouths," I said as I laughed. "You know I'm a germ freak. Gross."

I knew ultimately she just wanted me to be happy. This meant being protective of me, like when girls called our home asking for me. If Mom answered the phone when a girl called, she would signal her annoyance by giving me the evil eye. With her face scrunching up, one eye raised, and her lips elongated, her tongue would hit the roof of her mouth and this long "sssssssssss" sound would come out. You could tell it was a shortened version of another salty Korean word.

The sound was a unique combination of disgust, irritation, and warning. I would normally just mimic her look and return the same sound right back at her, causing her to erupt in laughter. She couldn't stay mad at me for long. I knew how to make Mom smile. After she'd hand me the phone, she'd walk away, trying to hold back her laughter and affectionately mumbling her normal Korean curse words.

My dad remained absent. The man who had once stood tall, full of confidence, now seemed reticent and unstable. Because he was gone, I was forced to take on adult roles when I was still immature. I struggled as I was in the height of my teenage years trying to still prove to myself that I mattered. The ongoing racism I experienced in Arizona, combined with the sense of betrayal from Dad, fueled an unhealthy performance mind-set, where I continually tried to prove people wrong. At the same time, my anger and resentment toward my father relentlessly kept growing. We felt abandoned as children.

As my mom observed my deteriorating relationship with my father, she was quick to say that the issues in our family were between him and her. Not between my father and us, the children. One day after I made a harsh comment about Dad, she pulled me aside, looked into my eyes, and spoke in a serious tone.

"Dabid, he's your father. No matter what, he's your dad."

I looked away for the moment and remained silent as she dramatically highlighted her comment with a long pause. Then she gave me that dramatic Korean stare to put an exclamation point on her admonition.

Mom felt my agony. Mom and I had this nonverbal connection. I don't ever remember having long conversations with her verbally, but I felt I could read what she was saying through her eyes. When she looked at me, she knew the internal mix of emotions waging a war inside me: hatred for my father for what he had done to her and my determination to protect her. My anger fueled a greater love for my mom and a stronger pressure to care for her.

"Mom, someday you won't have to work anymore," I had told her back in fourth grade. "I'll buy you some nice fur coats. I've got you." Fur coats weren't politically incorrect at the time but they were a symbol of extravagant luxury, which I felt my mom deserved. It was me saying, *I'll take care of you. You'll never have to worry again. You deserve it, Mom.*

The big question hanging over my head was who would take care of me. I was part of a mixed-race family that had imploded. Stigmas were associated with being a child of divorce. The Christian sentiment was that the likelihood of you becoming like your parents was high. My parents' divorce proved to the racists that people should stick to their own color. I didn't just hear that from white people; I heard it from Asians as well. Many thought people should stay within their own culture. And the truth was, even among some of my Korean elders, I knew that it was considered a shame to be with someone who didn't come from an honorable, respected whole family.

From a pragmatic perspective, who was going to help advise me through some of the hurdles of picking a university, a career, and a life partner? Who was going to provide a safety net if something went awry? The feelings of loneliness kept growing. My sister, brother, and I weren't close enough to try and figure it out together. Mom was savvy, but she didn't know the nuances of American culture or have the access to things Dad did simply because he was white. I know Mom was concerned about me as I was soon to leave the nest and venture to college.

I didn't recognize that Dad didn't have a safety net, either. He had once taught in our church, but after his affair, he was disgraced. At the time, I didn't consider how much he was going through but he must have walked around carrying a heavy load of shame. Once a popular leader whom all the young adults adored at church, he was now an outcast. He knew the rules. He never showed up at City Church again.

Coming back to church and the City Academy seemed oddly comforting, considering the chaos of my family life. The strict rules reminded me of the two-a-day football practices in the summer where people yelled at you. Like our football coach, the school's leaders were testing us to see if we could conform to the strict discipline and rules without complaining. The leaders knew it would build our character. Their motto was "No griping tolerated." Like football, there was a chain of command and penalties for doing something wrong.

I went back to City Academy with a renewed determination to excel despite the legalistic culture. Eventually I graduated "Most Improved Student." I don't remember studying that much. My class had around twenty graduates, which made the peer pressure and identity challenges more manageable. Mom showed up at my graduation in her finest dress. On special occasions such as this one, Mom put on makeup with her special perfume. She traded the high platform shoes from work for more fashionable high heels that made her taller. She would always sit about midway back in the auditorium, usually by herself. And no matter where she was, if I was speaking or getting recognized, Mom was there.

As I stood with the other students in our graduation regalia, my tassel flopping around and the cardboard graduation cap barely fitting my large head, I saw Mom. Inevitably, Mom started to softly cry. She always cried at our performances or when we were recognized for any achievement. It made me cry, too, because I knew this was one of her dreams for me.

Dad was a no-show. Who knows why? There was never an explanation.

Mom's next dream was for me to go to a university; I would be the first of our family to graduate from one. I already had my college picked out. There had been a clear choice from the moment I began to visit campuses, seeking to find the best place for my future. Many Asian parents envision their children going to Harvard, or any Ivy League school. To go to a community college or even a state college would be an utter failure. One parent I know named their child "Harvard" and another parent called her daughter "Mercedes" because this was their aspiration for their kids. Education was considered the ticket to success. Asian parents sacrificed prestigious jobs and friendships in Korea and took on work as custodians and small business owners in American urban neighborhoods considered dangerous at the time, so that their children would have the best opportunity to succeed. They bravely immersed themselves in unfamiliar cultures that were challenging to navigate with little English proficiency and cultural understanding.

When it came to selecting colleges, we were taught by our Christian leaders to be extremely careful about avoiding a "secular" school, which would be too "worldly" or liberal for us. Secular colleges, we were reminded, promoted communism and big government, which we believed would lead to the one world government that would rule and control all of us in the future. We would slide down the slippery slope of secularism and ultimately move away from God. All these negative things were considered signs of the end times. With the real discussion of a nuclear arms race with Russia and the culture of apocalypse from the Christian world I grew up in, it was no wonder my nightmares and paranoia continued into adulthood. I always felt this underlying anxiety of death. The belief was that as time moves on, the world continues to get increasingly worse. Apocalypse literally awaits us. While Mom may have understood some of these theological points, in her reality she had already survived the Korean War and poverty, discrimination and now a divorce, and she was resolute to at least see us succeed. She would sacrifice her life for ours.

Every Christian high school had colleges coming by to recruit students. During our senior year, we visited possible schools. Bob Jones University in Greenville, South Carolina, stood at the top of the list. It was the school that speaker Bud Bierman came from—the one who spoke at the camp in Telluride, Colorado. At the time it was the largest Christian university in the United States. It was considered the West Point of evangelicals, with the discipline, military culture, and rules to match. During our school tour, we were impressed by everything we saw. The university seemed well organized, and the student body looked mature, cool, positive, and purposeful. The clean-cut, freshly shaved, youthful energy seemed physically palpable as you walked throughout the campus. Well-manicured trees and green lawns felt like a utopian dream for students from a small Christian academy in barren Arizona.

The large student body wasn't the only reason Bob Jones stood out above the rest. The school had academic street cred and legitimate bragging rights. BJU always ranked at the top of the debate, speech, and musical competitions, competing sometimes with prestigious schools. Bob Jones required the students to take public speaking courses and attend both operas and Shakespearean plays every semester. Then there were chapels every weekday and on Sundays. Even though they were strict with rules, they seemed solid with their liberal arts education. They even boasted having the world's largest sacred art museum in the Western Hemisphere, filled with works by renowned artists. As students, our orientation included lessons on how to eat properly at mealtime and how to appropriately interact with other students, including possible marriage partners. There was a no physical contact rule that students bristled about but parents appreciated. Some called it the "6-inch rule."

This leads us to one more reason we were interested in Bob Jones that none of us acknowledged but everyone knew. Where we grew up, the goal was to get married as soon as possible so you wouldn't "burn in your lusts." Many of my friends got married right out of high school. Going to college meant I was getting married late! My hormones were raging. It was appropriate then to enroll in the schools where the best opportunities for possible meaningful relationships were. Since Bob Jones University was the biggest Christian university in America at the time, it felt like a no-brainer for me. My numerical odds were best at BJU.

I wanted to be different than my parents. To prove to myself and to others that a marriage can last, grow in love, and even be interracially partnered and thrive. When I finally decided to attend Bob Jones University, Mom couldn't have been prouder. She didn't know much about the Christian school except that it was a respected university that those we surrounded ourselves with at the church highly recommended and revered.

Soon after arriving on campus, I mailed Mom a postcard with a grand picture of the school showing its multicolored fountains at night and a large auditorium in the background. I wanted her to know how great the school was. I knew she was proud of me even though she would never tell me. Like any of the letters or postcards I sent her, my note was brief and written in big letters so I didn't have to write much. Like with our phone calls, I wasn't one to use many words.

Mom, I miss you. I love you! Your son, Dave.

I knew the words themselves didn't matter. Not to Mom. Some things can't be described in words. The main thing I wanted her to know was that I was working on her American dream.

CHAPTER TWELVE

Grits and Gravy

Three days after arriving at Bob Jones University, I had no doubt I was truly in the Deep South. I discovered a rule I had vaguely heard about called the No Interracial Dating Policy, which specified that you could not date anyone outside your race. I didn't investigate this as I thought it wouldn't apply to me at all because of my biracial roots. Since I was half-white and half-Korean, I had assumed I would be able to choose my race. The identifiable races to them were Caucasian or white, Black, and Asian. East Indians were considered white. At the time, I was so self-absorbed and overly concerned about my well-being, I didn't even consider how my Black brothers and sisters were experiencing injustice. The racism they experienced was far more discriminatory and brutal. Very few Black people chose Bob Jones University. And among the very few Asians who did, none would dare challenge this No Interracial Dating Policy.

When I arrived, I realized that my understanding of this rule could be wrong. I felt the need to verify that this was indeed a legitimate rule but that it did not apply to me. With trepidation and rising anxiety, I rushed to my adviser's office in the morning before classes began. I felt a sense of panic suffocating me.

I came all this way to go to college with my friends and I might not even be able to date someone who doesn't look like me?

Sure, City Church and City Academy had rules that I questioned, like no rock music or going to Hollywood movies, but they never pulled the race card. I had experienced racism and prejudice during the fourth grade in public school and generally everywhere I'd go in public in Arizona all my life, but not in what I considered my church family.

My assigned adviser, Dr. Boyd, was an older Hebrew scholar and Old Testament theology professor. Always hunched over a little, he wore thick plaid jackets accompanied by a tie, and spoke in a deep voice with a Southern drawl. He was a man with a large presence, always a bit disheveled with his glasses and whiskers. He was brilliant and seemed like one of those curmudgeonly type of professors, the ones who always look like they're in pain about having to teach freshman newbies like me. His presence was intimidating as he had this perpetual scowl.

I knocked on his door.

"Come in," he said in his resonant bass tone. He turned his large wooden chair away from his desk to face me. Forced a look of interest. "What can I do for you, Mr. Gibbons?"

"Thank you for meeting with me, Dr. Boyd. I don't want to waste your time. I just had a question about the No Interracial Dating Policy. Does it apply to me because my dad is white and my mom is Korean? He's my genetic birth father. I know I look one hundred percent Korean, but my biological dad is white."

A huge smile went across my face. "Well, Dave, I don't think it's a problem since you are half-white and half-Korean."

Whew...I was so glad to hear that. Oddly, I wasn't even considering how ridiculous this conversation sounded.

I walked out of there but wanted to make doubly sure. I didn't want to be expelled from school for breaking a rule. There was a reason they called this the West Point for Christians. It was a highly regulated environment. Demerits were handed out for not making your bed or talking past the lights-out bell at 11 p.m., holding hands with your girlfriend, or being late for a required event. There was a check-in system for going out and for coming onto the campus. If you got 100 demerits, you'd get permanently campused for the semester, which meant you couldn't leave the gated grounds. In certain circumstances, you could even be expelled for a 150 demerits or some other nonnegotiable rule like dating interracially.

Being extremely sensitive to rules and not wanting to waste my mom's hard-earned money for me to attend school, I wanted to be confident there would be no issues with this policy. I went to the dorm supervisor to affirm what Dr. Boyd had told me. Dorm supervisors oversaw a hierarchy of student leaders assigned to each dorm room. I met with him and explained to him my situation, just like I did Dr. Boyd, and he agreed that I was good. I was half-white and half-Korean. That's what mattered, not my physical appearance. Yes! I was in. But still embarrassingly insensitive to the plight of others in similar circumstances. I was raised in this "No griping tolerated" culture. You learned not to challenge authority, which would be a sin.

⌁

Before the conservative evangelical leader Jerry Falwell founded Liberty University, there was Bob Jones University. Bob Jones Sr., a well-known evangelist who was one of the predecessors of Billy Graham, founded the university in 1927 because he wanted to combat what he believed was a compromising and lackadaisical generation rising. He and others like him felt that the world was becoming too liberal when it came to their beliefs about evolution, the Bible, sex, sexuality, and who you associate with. Hence, the evolution of what is known among this subculture of Christians as the Fighting Fundamentalists grew larger. Or as some would quip: No Fun, too much Damn, and No Mental. Falwell himself would launch a political force called "The Moral Majority." Ostensibly, the vision at Bob Jones was to establish a training center for youth that would be known for its "academic excellence, refined standards of behavior, and opportunities to appreciate the performing and visual arts." There was a real emphasis on culture and civility, as well as old-fashioned Southern etiquette and the performing arts.

The school liked to advertise themselves as "The World's Most Unusual University." And many would agree. You could feel the energy of all these private school students and homeschoolers from around the nation coming together to discover people just like them. We were the new wave of conservatives battling for what was right. Conservative religiously and politically. To some, Bob Jones was treated as a reform school or a place to get you on the straight and narrow. The hope of many parents was that their young prodigies would "get their lives back together again" and, of course, find a godly life partner to marry. There was always a group of students who did not want to be there; they had been forced to go there. It was like a recovery house for rebels. To me, this was like Bunt's camps or two-a-day football practices. I could take the heat. Even if I couldn't agree with the rules or the demerit system, I knew doing things that I didn't like doing would be good for my character. That's how I had been taught to reason when I didn't agree with authority. I felt the discipline would strengthen who I was. It actually felt oddly comfortable coming to a place of rules. Coming from chaos, structure and order were a relief.

I discovered that those who were attending Bob Jones from Korea loved the school because of its strict culture. Korean culture during this time was hierarchical, disciplined, formal, passionate, strong, and male-centric. When Korean parents heard about Bob Jones, they loved it because it was more like their own moral standards than their children's. The structure and the respect for authority aligned with Korean parents' values. I don't think my mom cared about that. She was just excited that I was going to college, period.

Bob Jones was in lockstep with the church culture I had grown up in during a time when authority and institutions were disrespected and when we were constantly told that the world was getting worse. *You have to fight for what is right at all costs and expect persecution*, they said. *Persecution means you're doing something right.* Fear was provoked to encourage us to do right. Women weren't allowed to wear pants publicly and skirts had to be beneath the knee.

Now that my fears about dating were put to rest, I dove into college life. I became a voracious reader, disciplining myself to a rigid schedule where I would rigorously organize times to study, work, hang out with friends, sleep, and even take fifteen-minute naps. If I was going to take care of my mom, I didn't want to waste her money. I wanted her to be proud of me. I could picture her in just four years, standing in this auditorium full of thousands of people, crying like she did when I graduated from high school. Her dream of marriage might have fallen apart, but her dream for me would come to fruition soon. I'd make her proud. I'd eventually work multiple jobs on campus and off, while still participating in intramural sports and, of course, dating women from around the country.

The dating scene at the school was exciting because there was a culture of meeting others without having to get serious. It was a dating paradise. Since there was a no-touch rule in place, the environment was considered safe by concerned parents.

Since the university encouraged dating and getting to know others, the Dining Common at BJU became one of the magical grounds for matchmaking. Where better to possibly meet the love of your life than while you're enjoying some good ol' Southern food—scrapple, sausage, bacon, meatloaf, mashed potatoes, butter, and gravy. Lots of gravy. Grits and gravy. Biscuits and gravy. Scrambled eggs and gravy. Country fried steak and gravy. The genius plan was to mix thousands of students from the different dormitories and assign them to specific tables to get to know others. If the stars aligned, you would get a shot with someone you normally would never have crossed paths with.

Just watching the sit-down dinners in the football field–length cafeteria was an awe-inspiring sight. After the prayer, you'd see streams of student servers swiftly making their way to their assigned tables to serve. It was a well-orchestrated feat done almost every day of the year. Every freshman was required to take etiquette lessons highlighting table manners, conversations, and treatment of others at the table. It did feel like a military academy.

During my first year, I was assigned to a table where I met one of the most beautiful young women I'd ever seen. Tall, with long sandy brown hair and an attractive smile, Rebecca Locklear stood out. However, the unique difference in her vibe was her kindness and humility. I knew she would be a great partner to do life with. I could just see it in her eyes and the way she carried herself. Her eyes were gentle and generous. She was energetic and walked with purpose.

Every dinner table had two hosts to keep the conversation going, and since Rebecca was friends with one of the hosts, she was relaxed and at ease. For several weeks we were able to talk and get to know each other better. While I conversed with everybody, it was hard not to pay special attention to Rebecca.

Over the course of many meals, I got to know details about Rebecca. She had grown up in rural northern Maryland. Like me, she'd come from a strict religious background, including a Methodist school where her mother, Mary, was a librarian. Mary grew up a tomboy with a father who built houses and liked using his tractor. The conservative Pentecostal church she attended deemed her not spiritual because she lacked the gift of tongues, which is when someone believed to have the Holy Spirit starts to speak in a heavenly or unknown language—unknown to us at least. It can sound like gibberish. But anyone who really knows Mary Locklear knows how close she is to God, evidenced by her tough yet gentle spirit, her wise spiritual insight, and her humble care of those who are suffering. Rebecca's dad's genetic roots were European and Lumbee Indian. He was a Navy seaman, physically fit with a darker complexion and strong chiseled features. After the Navy, he joined a local construction company, where he died in a tragic construction accident, leaving behind his wife, two sons, and Rebecca. All the children were very young at the time. Becca was long-suffering and patient. She carried the no-frills attitude of her mother, and the tenacity and resilience of her father. As I got to know her, I could tell that she had also inherited the strong moral compass of both parents and their deep spirituality.

After a few weeks, students would rotate tables at the Dining Common to meet new people. After we'd said our good-byes for the last sit-down meal together, I waited a couple minutes for the table to exit and then surreptitiously looked at this index card–size list of names of those who'd sat at our dinner table this time around. I found Rebecca's dorm and room number. After jotting them down, I went back to my room and proceeded to write her a note to ask her out.

At this time, the only way we could formally ask a young woman out was either face-to-face or, more popularly at this school, via the nightly letter run between the men's and women's dorms. There's an art to taking the time to write a letter to someone on a piece of stationery. You get an understanding of who the person is, by not just the words, but also their handwriting, their pictures, and the fragrances they add to their letters. You had to put your note in the box by a set time. Then the men's literary societies took turns running boxes of notes from dorm to dorm. Once the letters got to the dorm, they were sorted by floors, and the dump would happen. They would throw all the letters in the middle of the dorm hall. Those who already had partners were the calm ones who were accustomed to regularly getting their notes. The people waiting to be asked out or those waiting for an answer from someone they wanted to go out with nervously retrieved their letters. Some would take their letters privately back to their rooms, while others would open them on the spot. You would hear shouts of joy or hear the moans of guys who got denied.

I had asked Rebecca to a soccer game on campus as a possible first date. My roommates had zero confidence in me.

"Gibbons, she's a sophomore and you're a freshman," they told me. "She's beautiful. She isn't going to say yes to you, son." "Son" was Southern slang we used to say to emphasize surprise or affirmation, or to be a bit derogatory in a friendly way. Although this term used with someone you didn't know could be a fighting word.

I didn't let the guys' skepticism hold me back. My attitude was always, *It doesn't hurt to ask.*

That night when study hall was over and the letters were arriving on the hall floors, I found a letter from Rebecca waiting for me. As I got to my room and tore open the letter, with my roommates watching in anticipation, I took the time to meditate on each word slowly, like every word was a prime cut of KBBQ. And there it was. The word I was looking for...

Yes.

Our first date at the soccer game was wonderful because it

rained. It allowed me to get closer to her under my umbrella. On a campus that didn't allow physical contact with your date, touching shoulders was a thrill. I didn't even care about the game. I was enthralled with Becca and the freedom of her laughter that night. Who doesn't like someone that laughs at all your jokes or humorous stories? She was at ease around me. And I was comfortable with her. I walked her back slowly to her dorm and couldn't believe how great the date had gone.

Rebecca would later tell me that, after our first date, she told people that I was "more American" than her. I was the first Asian person she'd ever met. Rebecca lived in a mostly white, rural area of Maryland, where gentlemen's farms picturesquely lined the forests, lakes, and hills. She added that I was "the most fun guy to date." And what was great about dating me was that I made her "comfortable around other guys."

In other words, I had launched Becca into a spectacular dating life where she would find someone else to be her boyfriend. In fact, when socially awkward or inept guys were anxious around her, she helped them to relax. Becca said she learned that from me. I had set her free! Good for her, but not for me.

For a while, I was asking Rebecca out as much as I could. I was ready to settle down. She would say yes every time initially. Then her letters began to change. "Sorry, I already have a date that night." She started being increasingly popular with the guys. It got to the point I had to ask her out months ahead for a date. Eventually I started seeing her around with this tall basketball player from Colorado. I saw how they were gazing into each other's eyes and I knew it was over for me. It was a look that you knew meant their relationship was serious. I took comfort in the fact that I had helped her dating life so that she could socially connect better with guys like this. Nah, I wasn't that righteous.

But I wasn't going to let this ruin my personal vibe. Because there were so many eligible candidates, if one person rejected you or cooled off, you learned to cope with it. Not take it too personally. You'd move on. I was only twenty years old but felt the clock ticking. People were getting married after high school. I felt I had no time to lose. My goal was to lock in my potential wife my freshman year. That way I'd be able to focus. But until then, I just had to keep trying. That's where my Asian roots showed up. It was a numbers game. While I didn't fit the Asian stereotype of loving math, I knew enough to recognize that the odds were in my favor.

So going out with me had bolstered Rebecca's confidence? No problem. Rebecca gave me confidence, too. At our school, the culture was set up so that dating was easy. They took away the pressure of trying to get someone into bed with you, because it was against the rules. Breaking any rules of physical contact could get you a ticket home. As a result, on dates, there wasn't any pressure to do anything physically. It was a gift not to have the expectation or pressure of being physical too quickly, at least to the parents. On a date, the focus was on the conversation you were having and who the person really was. I had fun getting to know different women. All of them were kind and enjoyable to be with.

Arriving back home after my freshman year at BJU, I hadn't forgotten about Rebecca. In fact, whenever I met with family and friends and showed them photos of my classmates in the annual yearbook, I would show them Rebecca's photo.

"Look here. This was the young woman I really liked. The one I thought was best for me. [*Sigh.*] But it didn't work out."

But the unimaginable can happen.

CHAPTER THIRTEEN

눈치 Nunchi— a Dark Premonition

Mom's going to die soon.

This premonition came to me without warning while I was driving back home after my freshman year at BJU. This strong, intuitive feeling that something unpleasant was about to happen came like a notice from a doctor who knew I would need some prep time for this dark potentiality.

But even more than a premonition, I attribute it to the Korean idea of "nunchi" (pronounced "noon-chee").

Nunchi, sometimes spelled noonchi (눈치), is a Korean concept reflecting the subtle ability to listen and perceive others' feelings, moods, or well-being. It first appeared in the seventeenth century as nunch'ŭi (眼勢 in hanja), meaning "eye force/power." In Western culture, some might liken nunchi to the concept of emotional intelligence. More than EQ—emotional quotient, which is another way to talk about emotional intelligence—it is the ability to see who and where a person is. You know that you know. I had that sense that Mom wasn't doing well. We had a soul connection. I sensed in unspeakable terms that Mom was in her last few months of life.

When I was a child, my biggest fear was of my parents dying. In my nightmares, I watched Mom and Dad dying in a variety of horrific ways. A house fire. A plane crash. A tsunami. In a world war. Or us being left behind at Christ's return. Each time, I woke up with my heart racing and then rushed to my parents' room, only to find them sleeping, but thankfully alive. Sometimes I headed back to my bed relieved while other times I jumped into their bed at the risk of disturbing them. I couldn't picture a life without my parents.

I grew up with this worry and always found it surprising that other kids didn't think this way. Yet even with those fears, I wasn't really trained to do anything differently. We weren't taught stress management or how to release anxiety by deep breathing techniques. I learned to simply live with these fears. This premonition and nunchi, however, went beyond fear to a strong sense that something bad was going to happen, specifically to my mom. And it was going to happen very soon.

I still vividly recall the breakdown she had one night shortly after my dad left. The words she told me in her thick accent still saddened me.

"Dabid—the only reason I'm alive is for you kids."

I knew I would never forget watching her cry and waiting for her to stop, then guiding her to her bedroom without saying a word.

Whether my premonition about her dying was real or not, I thought it a good thing to forgo the normal time with friends and instead spend extra time with Mom that summer. I was determined to spend this next summer with her as if it was her last summer on earth. I was going to try and cherish each moment with her. When I got home from school, I let her know my intentions:

"Hey, Mom, I want to hang out with you more this summer."

"왜 Why?"

Mom found it peculiar that I would want to be with her since I loved going out and hanging with my friends.

"Because I like you, Mom."

"아이구 Aigoo," she replied.

Aigoo was a lighthearted way of saying, "Oh geez," or OMG. Her face wore a forced frown, but underneath it was a clear smile.

That summer I frequently caught myself staring at her.

It took me a while to get accustomed to her new wrinkles, the proliferation of gray hairs, and a slight extra little chin. In the past I'd usually tease her about such things, but not anymore. Mom felt more fragile. Besides, these small changes never detracted from her beauty; each sign of aging made her more uniquely endearing. Each wrinkle was a beautiful reminder of how she'd persevered and endured so much. I grew up accustomed to seeing this strong, petite Korean woman filling a room with her energy. Yet I could tell that spark was slowly fading. I would gaze at her eyes when she wasn't looking and notice that they had dimmed. Mom's eyes once danced with life but now seemed lost without hope. It felt like Mom was drowning in her sorrows, barely surviving.

I tried to place myself in her situation as a middle-aged woman, Korean, and divorced. In the patriarchial world of our church community, she didn't have relationships beyond my father's network. The church was a man's domain. The faithful wife was expected to support, respect, and submit to her partner. With my dad now gone, so were all the relationships she was accustomed to when it came to our family. She still had some friends at work, but her home was her place of joy. Seeing her family together, laughing with all these Americans was for her a dream achieved. Now it was gone.

I didn't understand the pain she must have endured until recently. I realized that as we were becoming adults, the idea of being alone in her older age must have haunted her. As loved ones died, life moved on. Friends disappeared or passed away. The fear of being alone must have been overwhelming. Is there a greater suffering than being abandoned and alone?

Even though Mom was still young, in her forties, she looked older. The Chevy incident was four years ago, but the impact of everything to follow had taken its toll. Her eyes told a story if you looked closely. From a distance they always appeared slightly swollen because of her constant flow of tears. Up close, they appeared hollow and numb. They carried this deep sadness. It was the han thing. Her gaze reflected her reality, a look of sad resignation to this damning plight she was enduring.

It wasn't just her eyes. Mom's voice sounded increasingly raspy, a consequence of starting to smoke again to calm her nervousness and anxieties. Her laughter was not as hearty, long, or deep. She used to laugh so hard, she'd fall and curl up in a ball, trying to contain her laughter. But now it seemed she was covering the pain that couldn't be lightened by humor. Her soul was overwhelmed in suffering. The controlled and suppressed outward behavior was her trying to show us she was okay. It became increasingly difficult for her to contain her sorrow. Her smiles became forced.

Eventually, Mom's routines became normalized after the divorce, but she was never the same. You could see she was just trying to survive each day. Her whole life in this country had been so intertwined with Dad's that she lost more than a husband when he left our family. She lost herself in his dreams and aspirations. She enjoyed seeing Dad get recognized or us kids achieving honors at school. She gladly faded into the backdrop of any scene. The man who brought her to America and provided access to her dreams was sleeping with someone else at night. Mom's nights were reminders of her loneliness when she crawled into her cold bed. Her evenings were spent trying to forget the pain from her broken relationship with my dad.

Her physical body mirrored her emotional state. She started to lose weight. She couldn't process many foods because of the ulcers in her stomach. The stress was taking a toll on her physically. I often heard Mom retching in her bedroom bathroom. With her health declining, she focused on working to sustain our family's needs. She started coming home for a little bit and would go out again to be with others at bars. It made me wonder if this was how she met men when she was younger in Korea.

I regret not being able to talk to her about her pain. I didn't know how to. And perhaps, I didn't want to. When the separation first occurred, I normally would just lose myself in music in my room or go out with my friends. I was nineteen years old. It became overwhelming, because the future was so certain and unstable. I let the ignominious pain find a dark hole in my soul and take residence there. I numbed my pain, trying to make myself feel more significant through sports, leadership, or academics. When I started to follow Christ, I found that significance in serving others. Church was a second home.

The voices Mom endured through the night were formidable, heavy, and constant. When she woke up, I could see the pain's effects on her face. She still looked tired, like she hadn't slept. As she aged self-doubt and the voices of her dark past grew louder. For Mom, that voice of joy and peace was silent. Her outer and inner worlds were ransacked by unforeseen circumstances and "irreconcilable differences." Slowly, Mom's love for life left her.

I wish I could have magically brought back Mom's natural optimism. But when Dad left, you could tell she lost hope, too.

Processing painful relationships like this wasn't really part of Mom's past. When things got bad, she would run. It was primal. She had to flee since no one was protecting her. Where was Mom going now? She thought about her own death. It probably would not have been the first time. She stayed alive for us kids. Knowing that made it worse for me. I felt guilty that I was never doing enough. As for the group of Christians we knew, they were well intentioned and good people but they weren't helpful in figuring out how to care for a middle-aged, divorced Korean immigrant woman. As children, we still had a support network in place, but Mom didn't.

This summer I would have opportunities to lead things at church and work with the children, but my main focus was Mom. I wanted to help her recover that spark again. If for no other reason, I wanted to be with her. She was home.

⌒৲

"I'll be waiting in the car," I told Mom as I went outside to start her old Mustang.

The sun was still hiding behind the horizon as I slipped into the blue vehicle and revved it to life. I enjoyed driving her to work even though it was 6:00 a.m. Mom wasn't a careful driver—she'd already gotten in a minor fender bender. She didn't learn to drive until late in life. She became that driver oblivious to other drivers, swerving across multiple lanes as people are honking their horns and shouting out spicy words. Middle fingers being thrust into the air. Quick stops. Frightening lane changes. No need to go to an amusement park. If you wanted a good scare, let my mom drive the car.

As she slipped into the seat next to mine, I was reminded of how much I loved being with her. It was comfortable to just sit with her and not say anything. I loved being near her because I could pick up her scent. She had that mom smell. It was a sweet, strong fragrance.

She didn't douse herself with expensive perfumes. Her natural aroma emanating from her body transcended any applied fragrance coming from the cosmetics she wore for the day. Her scent reminded me of warm chestnuts and cocoa. Unless she ate kimchee with rice. Then you could smell the fresh garlic cloves. Still, it was comforting and peaceful.

It was a fifteen-minute drive to her workplace called A Hair Affair. In the car, I'd reach across the gear shift and hold Mom's hand as the stereo played her songs. She liked the old Korean folk-style songs that sounded like somebody was in pain. The kind of songs that didn't sound festive, but more like someone was lamenting. The vibrato was long and agonizing. I wish I could have belted out some of the Korean songs she enjoyed. The sorrowful Korean voices communicated the type of suffering that comes from the depths of your soul. While I didn't know any of those Korean songs, I knew she loved the hymns from church. Those old spiritual hymns brought her comfort.

Seeing the town come to life on our morning drive brought back a childhood memory.

"Remember when I used to get up at five in the morning to go deliver the newspapers?" I asked Mom.

She gave me a knowing smile as she nodded.

Mom and I would wake up at the same time during my middle school years. Occasionally, Mom would help me to pack my newspapers in the bins on my bike to deliver to our neighbors. A bundle of *Arizona Republic* newspapers would be dropped off at my house to prepare for delivery to all my customers in the neighborhood. I'd cut the binding, fold the papers, encircle them with a rubber band, and carefully tuck them into the side bins on my bicycle. On Sundays, I would make two trips back to my house because the papers were so thick, they couldn't all fit in one trip. My ability to loft the papers behind walls and angle them into the door from the street was what helped me later to become a softball pitcher with pinpoint accuracy. Pitching softballs was easy compared to throwing newspapers behind jutting walls and fences while dogs were chasing you. Occasionally, if I lost focus, I would hit a window or two, but nothing ever broke.

"Whenever I got up too late, you would be outside folding the papers for me," I reminded Mom.

"I liked to see you collecting money from customers," she told me.

That was just like her.

The paper route was followed by my first jobs as a teenager working at McDonald's, and then at State Farm Insurance as a filing clerk. I inherited my hustle from my mom. It's the *I'll outwork you* mind-set. The type of attitude that thinks, *I might not be the fastest or the brightest but I'll outlast you.*

I could still picture those occasional mornings as a middle schooler in the cool crisp desert air before sunrise. I loved how it was just the two of us getting a head start before the rest of the world. We wouldn't say much to each other as we were folding the newspapers and carefully positioning them in the basket, but the connection between us always flowed. "Mom, thanks for giving me a hand." She'd slowly get up from her crouched 아줌마 halmoni/grandma position folding papers and smile. I know she loved that I was working so hard.

During this morning drive, like all of them, we didn't talk much. I didn't say the things in my heart. Like Mom, I didn't always articulate how I felt. Hopefully my actions translated into what Mom could understand.

That summer, whether we were eating, watching TV together, or going to the mall, I would just walk with her side by side, trying to soak her in. She'd still let me hold her hand even though I was now a college student. I'd worry, thinking how I was going to be able to care for her as she aged. What would her life be like down the road? When she passed away, would I forget the details of her face? Would I remember the fragrance of her perfume and makeup mixed with the scent that was uniquely hers?

People talk about others lighting up a room. Mom was the sun and the moon when she walked in. Day or night, Mom could shine. When Mom showed up, you knew she was present, ever watchful, breaking down what was happening. She was adept at surveying and assessing as a young adolescent in postwar Seoul. These skills helped her to navigate her unfamiliar surroundings. She had successfully adapted with the harsh conditions and rapid changes in Korea. She had a winsome, natural beauty and an ease about her that people felt drawn to. She styled hair for elite influencers and entertainers as well as her everyday customers. People knew Mom as a generous person. Mom gave to those around her constantly. While she had opinions of people, I rarely heard her say a disparaging thing about anyone.

On the final day of the summer break, as I was set to drive once again with my close friends cross-country to Bob Jones University, the same thought that had been playing on an infinite loop inside my head throughout the summer became a reality.

What if THIS is my last day with Mom?

After getting up early and getting ready to make myself present-able for the long trip back to school, I thought of the salon she worked at. A Hair Affair. The word "Affair" triggered me. It used to mean nothing to me, but now it was a reminder of what had happened between Mom and Dad. This thought dissipated as Mom walked into the room, looking good as always in her fresh uniform top. Her high platform shoes made her four inches taller and her makeup was on point. Lips freshly plumped up and large false eyelashes in place.

Mom and I made the walk to the car in our driveway in the darkness of the morning. She held her cup of coffee as I loaded her brushes, stored in a large pink plastic container, in the car, along with her metal money box, to organize all the checks and cash from her customers. As we drove down Superstition Freeway, I took her hand once again, and held it tightly. These were the hands that had once cradled me, washed me, combed my hair, and changed my diapers. I found myself glancing at her hands. Her hands had labored for decades ever since she was young. Now they were getting wrinkled and chapped from all the chemicals used to wash, condition, perm, and color hair. The beauty industry wasn't as careful then about harsh chemicals as they are today. I thought about her life. Who she was. The things I knew and didn't know about her. The abject poverty she had emerged from as a child. An alcoholic father who died when she was still young. The Korean soldier she ran away with. Meeting my father, the young, suave Midwesterner. Getting married. Having us kids. And then the divorce.

I had so many questions about her past. Mom never brought up the early years of her life because she was more focused on our future. About making it in America. She was determined we would live differently than she had. Her joy would be our successes.

As we arrived at the shop in the early morning, I let go of Mom's hand and rushed to open the backseat to help her with her brushes she had brought home and cleaned overnight. She was always the first one to arrive at the salon. As the top beautician working at A Hair Affair, she was favored by the owner. He was a vibrant, rotund middle-aged white man with sandy blond permed hair and a nicely groomed mustache and beard. He depended on my mom to bring her magic to the space and the customers.

I followed Mom into the store with the bin of brushes and set them in the corner spot, where her customers would sit to get their hair done. Even though I was becoming a man, I still felt more like her child in this moment. Mom's platform shoes clapped the floor as she walked. The styling chairs in front of the row of mirrors reminded me of barber chairs, but thinner and more elegant. As always, I caught the scents of familiar chemicals used to color or give perms. Mom's chair was in the favored spot, right in the middle of the action where she could impact the whole room. On the counter and the wall were pictures of us kids. She loved to tell stories about us and our accomplishments, either academically or in sports. So many of her customers told me how Mom proudly spoke about us.

As I placed her pink container of brushes down, I felt the tears starting to fill up my eyes. I'm not good with good-byes. I cry watching commercials. So early on, I made it a point never to say "good-bye" to my loved ones. Saying "good-bye" always felt too final to me.

As I looked Mom in the eyes, I gathered myself and unconsciously took a deep breath to get the words out.

Just be quick or you'll be a complete wreck and Mom will wonder what's wrong, I told myself.

"Mom, I love you," I said. "I'll see you real soon."

As tears streamed down my face, I kissed her on the cheek and gave her a big hug, knowing this might be the last time I embraced my mom while she was alive. I held her tightly.

On the verge of doing one of those ugly cries, I quickly turned and briskly walked toward the door. After I got back into the Mustang, I sat there looking into the salon. I couldn't hold the tears anymore now streaming down my face. The shop was brightly lit, a golden glow emanating into the dark of the morning. It was quiet and still. Mom standing alone. She bowed her head and wiped away her tears. Like me, she held back most of her tears until we were out of each other's sight.

For a moment, I couldn't move. I could barely breathe. I just looked at her as my tears flowed. When I gathered myself, I whispered to her as if she could still hear me.

"Mom, I'll see you real soon." I sat there with tears still streaming down my face. I bowed my head. I paused and took one last look at her.

Deep down, I could feel the vast emptiness growing inside of me as I thought about Mom not being home anymore.

CHAPTER FOURTEEN

Hit and Run

As my sophomore year began, I was reminded how wonderful it was to see the flourishing green landscapes of the South and then watch the vast fields and hills covered with trees as their leaves showed off their array of fall colors. The transition from summer to fall is more vivid in South Carolina than Arizona. The leaves on the trees signal to you that fall is near.

My goal this year was to pour myself into my studies, but more important, it was to be a social butterfly. I wanted to live out what a wise mentor had once shared with me:

"The most important thing is not the education you'll gain from college. You won't remember what your teachers said. What's the most important thing about your university experience is to learn how to live."

That made sense to me. For me, school was about developing good habits of scheduling, work, and rest, and of course, great friendships. My freshman year was under my belt. I felt more confident going into this year. I was able to date and feel free from much of the worries at home. The busyness of school doesn't leave time for idleness.

Now in my second year, I gained traction as a leader on campus. I got a job checking men in and out as they left the school grounds. Since Bob Jones was like a military academy, and there were strict rules about when and why you could leave the campus. I became one of the operational gatekeepers of the student body, interacting with men daily. Working at the main reception desk to the world of the school, I met almost every male student in the dormitories. I enjoyed making new friendships and acquaintances. I was soon elected class officer, probably because people regularly interacted with me. In high school I rarely studied much, but in college I was getting into a groove for how to learn. I was studying multiple hours a day. I wasn't that stereotypical Asian kid who went to school and then worked with tutors after school. Playing on football and baseball fields was more important to me than crunching numbers.

But here, studying came easier. I was becoming increasingly convinced I was going to be a pastor, preferably at some large church where I could raise a family and comfortably settle down. I didn't want to suffer. My ambition was to cultivate a community that wouldn't give up on each other. My challenge would be learning the Greek and Hebrew languages and, of course, taking speech classes. I always got nervous when I spoke publicly. In my first required speech class in college, I remember standing before my class of about twenty students and the extraordinarily talented Professor Jeffrey Arthurs. I was introduced. Students had their evaluations on their desks ready to critique me. And I went BLANK. I totally forgot what I was going to say. I remember awkwardly looking at the teacher. Looking at the students in the class, I said:

"I don't remember what I'm supposed to say."

I was so embarrassed. It's every speaker's nightmare.

Part of college life is dealing with the challenges that come with higher learning.

The challenge I didn't want to enter into was now becoming reality.

⌒

It was October 6, early in the school year. I remember that the sun was spectacularly bright. Blue skies. Fresh, crisp cool air. Autumn leaves floating to the ground. You could hear the birds up in the trees. Students hurried to the next class clutching books in their arms and freshly typed papers in their briefcases and tote bags. Some were literally running because they were going to be late otherwise.

As I was on my way to a class, someone darted toward me from the direction of the dorms.

"Dave, Dave!"

It was Dennis, my first-year roommate. Dennis was a gifted classical pianist. He'd won competitions all his life and was now majoring in piano performance. Clean and proper, Dennis was meticulously dressed at all times. He had wavy brown hair carefully combed and sprayed. He was always measured and composed in his movements and speech. His pronunciations were exacting and precise, like the way he played his classical music. I don't know how he constantly managed the piano performance pressure from an early age. But his talent was exceptional and his heart kind.

I had never seen Dennis looking as distraught as he did now. He looked worried.

As he reached me and stood there out of breath, he said, *"Dave, your sister just called. It's an emergency. You have to call her back."*

At that time we didn't have cell phones. We only had a wall phone in each of our dorm rooms. I ran straight back with Dennis to the room. I dialed my sister's number. Chong picked up the phone. There was a long pause, and then Chong burst into tears. She couldn't speak. Usually her voice was always distinct and bright; she learned to speak this way by working as a receptionist at a large Caterpillar machinery plant in Arizona. Now she was crying, unable to speak, fighting to catch her breath between sobs.

I braced myself because I'd never heard my sister weep like this. Something tragic must have happened.

"Chong, what's wrong?" I softly asked.

"Mom...was killed last night in a hit-and-run accident."

She could barely say it before her grief overwhelmed her. I could tell her whole body was shaking just by the way she sounded.

Earlier that morning, my sister had woken to men pounding on the front door. When Chong opened the door, she saw they were Arizona highway patrol officers, flashlights in hand. They had asked if she was Debbie (Son Chae) Gibbons's daughter. Chong, bewildered, still coming out of deep sleep, said, "*Yes.*"

"I'm sorry to inform you of this, but your mom was killed last night in a hit-and-run accident."

I can envision Chong slumping to the floor, overwhelmed by every child's worst nightmare.

The police report said that Mom had mechanical problems in the blue Mustang I'd driven her to work in just about a month earlier. She was driving on Interstate 10 that night in Phoenix. After pulling over into the emergency lane, she stepped out of her vehicle. As Mom walked down the emergency lane, seeking help, a truck swerved into Mom, crushing her. The driver of the truck stopped for a moment, then saw what had happened and sped off, dragging my mom a distance on the freeway.

A highway patrol officer witnessed what happened. He reported seeing the whole incident, as he was behind the man who hit Mom. He was going to pursue the man who careened into Mom, but the priority was to give immediate medical assistance to her. The officer pulled over to attend to her. By the time he reached her and checked her pulse, Mom was gone. And so was the man who killed her. There was no license number. No identification. Soon the local news media was on-site, reporting the incident statewide. The officer shared that, most likely, the driver of the other car was intoxicated.

I can't imagine how my twenty-six-year-old sister managed the news she received during those early morning hours. The shock and horror slowly set in as Chong wilted to the floor and wept. Her only advocate. Her safe place gone.

As I held the phone, Chong was still sobbing in the background. Pastor Bunt, who was with her, came on the phone and said something, but I couldn't hear anything from that point on. I was in a state of shock and disbelief, even though I'd had that premonition.

The day turned into a blur. When the worst happens, your body goes numb. You're trying to process what is real and what is not. You're shocked the world didn't stop. How could life keep going on like normal—my mom just died!

My friends and classmates would later tell me that the announcement in the chapel on the campus that day was about me going home to my mom's funeral after the hit-and-run accident. I received many cards, notes, and gifts from the student body. One of these was from a close friend since childhood and roommate, Kevin Schaal. When he heard the news of my mom's death, he wrote this poem. I read it on the plane ride back home.

NIGHT

The sky I view contains no touch of blue
The signature of God's controlling reign.
Even for gray sky eyes now search in vain.
Oh, Lord, where is thy hand so blest and true,
To rescue me from agonizing hue,

Or this my life with sorrow ever stain.
Tis night I view that weighs down so my soul
Tis night that scared away the day
And with the day a loved one's soul away.
Now my empty soul views sky so black as coal.
My Lord, can ever again come the day?
Son, sit and ponder what's been done, is now the sky
     black or deepest blue?
Lord, it is the latter that is true.
Is my sovereign power then all gone,
Oh, Lord no, all that happens is by you.
And what more do you see way up on high?
I see a sparkling star there shining bright
That never I would see if not the night.
Yes, son, the wondrous star I placed on high
Is the reason for which I brought the night.

As I sat there on the plane and stared at the clouds through the window, I wept. The dark nights I'd felt from the day my mom locked herself in that Chevy kept turning in my mind. The tragic nature of my mom's death wrecked me. I couldn't see any light during this night. The darkness of the night rolled over me.

⁓

The chapel was packed with Mom's loyal customers, friends from church, and many people I didn't know. It was standing room only, and people overflowed into the lobby. My sister, brother, and I sat in the front row. Noticeably absent was my father. Absent from my graduation, absent now. Why would I expect anything different? The day that Mom died, on October 6, 1981, was Dad's first wedding anniversary with his new wife, Carolyn—the woman he'd had an affair with and left Mom for. It seemed like a sad irony, or at the least poetic justice. I felt awful for even thinking such a thing.

Prior to the service, I quietly went back to the side room, where Mom was lying in state. It was surreal seeing her in the ornate shiny beige casket. She lay there in a royal blue dress, her eyes closed. She wore the necklace and rings my sister had found in Mom's jewelry drawer. Makeup was caked on her skin to cover the bruises and traumas of the accident. It didn't look natural at all. Her hands were obviously badly contused, folded over her body. These were the hands I had tenderly caressed just a few weeks earlier.

As I leaned in closer to her, I started to lose it again. The worst fears I'd had as a child were now realized. I kissed her cheek, like I had done a thousand times since I was little. Yet this time there was no warmth. No smile. No laughter. There was no response from Mom. Just the cold smell of a funeral home, excessive makeup, and death.

I remember thinking it was odd to see the funeral staff so comfortable around death. When someone so significant to you dies, it's odd to see people carrying on with normality. There's a personal reality check that life has literally stopped yet the world moves on. The living are quickly forgotten. I was even struggling to see the details of Mom's face in my mind.

We buried Mom in Scottsdale, Arizona. My sister asked me to provide the words for her tombstone. How do you summarize a person's life in a few words? You see the digits of a person's birth and their death but that dash in between is filled with countless stories and people known and unknown. Pondering what to say, I remember what I prayed for Mom after her challenges with Dad. I prayed that she would experience joy again. Then it dawned on me that death was probably the only way my mom would ever get over her sorrow. She couldn't get past the divorce. I settled on the phrase "Joy in His Presence" because all her life she was searching for joy. I know in her lifetime she had experienced joy meeting Dad, having us kids, making her clients feel beautiful. I had resigned myself to the reality that Mom would never recover from the wounds of her life. I couldn't solve her problems. I couldn't heal her. This wasn't something I could fix. The thought of her being with God gave me some consolation, but the cruel reality of death lingers and doesn't move on quickly.

You never get over the loss of someone you love. It's an endless cycle of suffering and longing, a visceral yearning to be with them again.

⌒⌒

After the memorial service, my siblings and I went back home. Most of the time, we didn't say much. I think we were still in a state of shock. The house felt so empty without Mom. She was the life and energy of our home. But we had to keep taking care of details we were unprepared for. There were so many little things that needed to get done, like taking care of the rest of the funeral arrangements and sorting through her possessions.

Organizing her personal belongings was a slow methodical process, which helped us to deal with our grief. Mom's best friend, Kim Ahjumma, came all the way from San Diego to be with us. She was the one who had babysat me when my parents still lived in Korea. She assured me every time I saw her, "Da-bid, I gave you my milk." Then she'd smile with a maternal gaze looking into my eyes. By saying I drank her milk, Kim Ahjumma was saying, *Hey, your mom and I are like sisters and you are like my literal son.* It was her reminder of the important position she had in our lives because of her friendship with

Mom. She was Mom's closest friend since her early years in Korea. No matter how awkward that was every time she brought up her nursing me, I laughed and felt grateful for her friendship with Mom. Kim Ahjumma was simply trying to say she was family. She and Mom had gone through so much. Kim Ahjumma herself came from abject poverty, too. She also suffered through a divorce with an American. When she had been taken to Japan as a child, she was forced to go to a Japanese elementary school, where the Japanese children called her terrible names you never forget. Kim Ahjumma rarely smiled unless Mom made her laugh or when she'd tell me I drank her milk. I wondered how much of her stoicism was her natural self, or was this who she became after the relentless teasing and bullying she endured as a child in Japan. Her presence was calming, as she was like a second mom to us. She would just look at us and cry. She'd look at me with earnest eyes, grab my hands, and hold them. Later she would cook us Korean food, sit down with us, and just stare at us with empathetic eyes. She'd sit in silence but her presence filled us with compassion and love. Without words, she wanted us to know she truly loved us and that Mom loved us. Having Kim Ahjumma with us brought all of us comfort. She and Mom were so close that I could feel Mom's presence through her.

"Da-bid, your mom really loved you, Chong, and Doug. She told me how much you changed when you came back from the camp.

"I still remember when your mom called me to let me know how different you were. You had bought her flowers. Da-bid, your mom loved you. She really loved you."

Through all this, Kim Ahjumma was like my mom and didn't speak ill of my dad. There was a love and respect for my father that I'm sure she caught from my mom.

The police let us know that they had the purse Mom had with her when she was killed. We picked up the box of her belongings from the police station, took it home, and opened it up. The purse had been dragged with her on the interstate freeway. The black leather was scratched and dirty. Broken glass spilled out of it. Her wallet, with credit and ID cards, was inside. At the bottom of the purse, I pulled out a postcard. I held it close to examine it. I couldn't believe it. It was the postcard I had mailed Mom at the beginning of my freshman school year. I was surprised Mom kept it. Chong saw me holding the card. She then told me, "Dave, Mom took that post-card to work every day to show her customers where you were going to school. She was so proud of you that you were attending college and excelling."

It was something I had written so quickly, without much thought, not knowing how much Mom would treasure it.

As I held it, I started shaking. The tears wouldn't stop.

In the days to follow, I kept asking with greater intensity, "When does this pain stop, God?" I had believed when I connected back to God in Colorado, things would be different. That perhaps my parents would even get back together again. I longed for that. Prayed for their reunion. Yet their relationship only got worse.

Eventually, my grief turned to anger again.

Why did You take her? Why didn't You take Dad?

I couldn't believe I even thought that. I couldn't understand why God had chosen to take the innocent one instead of the one I thought was guilty. It was a horrible thing even to consider but I found my mind would often go to this dark place of what I thought would be justice.

I still kept Dad at a distance. I was probably trying to protect myself from any more pain. He was a no-show to me. He didn't show up to my graduation, and he didn't show up to Mom's funeral even to comfort us kids. I blamed Dad for everything that had happened. It wasn't fair that she had gotten what it seemed he deserved.

Mom was gone. I was trapped in a vicious cycle of sorrow that wouldn't end.

The question that Mom had kept asking me when I held her in my arms that late night: "Why?"

That was now my question.

CHAPTER FIFTEEN

No Interracial Dating

My heart started to pound. I stared at the small green piece of paper in my hand. I knew I was in trouble. This was the one note you don't want to see in your mailbox.

Toward the end of my sophomore year, as I checked my PO box on campus, like I did every other day, I discovered the dreaded green slip of paper from the Dean of Men's office.

Go to the Dean of Men's office immediately.

If you got that piece of mail, you knew it was bad news. I tucked the slip into my pants pocket in disbelief while preppy students in loafers collected their mail from the muted gray metal mailboxes lining the walls around me. My heart continued to beat wildly. I could be expelled. But for what? I had never been in any trouble with the school before. It could really be only one thing.

Filled with anxiety, I walked down the sidewalk. I arrived at the administration building, a beige brick building in the center of the campus. I felt like I was entering the White House as I passed old oil paintings of different university presidents and administrators lit up by a lot of brass lighting. I made my way up the stairs and arrived at the Dean's office. With my heart pounding, I knocked on his door.

"Come in," Dr. Milton said with a raspy voice, probably from preaching hundreds of fiery sermons over his forty-plus years of life.

His frame was lean under his dark suit. He came off as a man of action. His courtesy smile morphed into a serious expression as he looked at me. His eyes were sober and now serious.

"Hello, Dr. Milton. I'm Dave Gibbons. I got this slip to come to your office right away."

His pronounced square jaw tightened as he glanced at his notes and then looked back up at me.

"Dave, it's been reported you've been dating Caucasian."

He was absolutely right. I had never dated someone who wasn't white. No prejudice against other ethnic women; it was just who I mostly grew up with in the communities where I'd lived. Perhaps subconciously it was me ultimately feeling like I was accepted here in America if I was dating a white woman.

I had prepared a response, because this was something that had been a lingering concern since I'd arrived at BJU my freshman year. I didn't know at this time, but there was a national story happening about Bob Jones University's No Interracial Dating Policy. All the major news outlets were reporting about this policy. Bob Jones University's policy was being challenged in the Supreme Court because of the university's tax-exempt status. The question was, could a tax-exempt institution have a policy, belief, or rule that discriminates because of race? The ramifications of this case would be huge, because it could potentially affect every nonprofit in the country. It was about the legality of believing what you want to regardless of the US government's approval. It was a fight that Christian leaders, like those at Bob Jones, were prepared to aggressively pursue, because they were ready to fight big government or any growing government assault on what they saw as our "Christian" beliefs and our "Christian" liberties.

With as much calm as I could muster, I responded to Dr. Milton: "I spoke to my dormitory supervisor and to my staff adviser, Dr. Boyd," I said. "They both said I could date Caucasian because I'm half-Asian and half-Caucasian."

"Well, you can't," Dr. Milton replied. "You look Asian, and you can only date those of your own race, which is Asian."

"Dr. Milton, I'm half-Korean and half-white. My mom is Korean and my dad is American, a white man."

"But you look a hundred percent Asian, Dave."

As worried as I'd been about being expelled before, I was strangely emboldened to question his beliefs now. Besides, he wasn't from the Deep South. I reasoned he should know better because he was from Colorado.

"Dr. Milton, how do you determine who can date who racially?"

He carefully measured his words as he said, "We determine who you can date by three things: your physical appearance, your language, and your primary culture."

"Well, two out of three is good," I said with a chuckle.

He didn't laugh.

"Dave—the bottom line is, you look Asian." Dr. Milton surprised me with his next comment. "Dave, we know you can cause significant trouble around here."

I had just been elected to a student body office where I shared a monthly inspirational talk to the whole sophomore class. I had also been recently elected to be the vice president of the ministerial class, the largest single major at BJU.

Dr. Milton paused for a moment and gave me a hard stare before continuing.

"In fact, you'll probably want to leave the school."

There were rumors saying that the national news media and the ACLU and others were looking for people internally, like a student or faculty member, to share their feelings about the No Interracial Dating Policy. Dr. Milton was in a tight situation with me because I was a public student body leader. He knew I could cause an unusual stir if students knew of my situation. My situation was unique because I was technically considered biracial genetically. Later, my brother, Doug, who looks more white than I do, joined me at BJU and was able to date white, even though we both believed we were genetically the same, having the same parents. There are many children who have biracial parents who look more like one parent than the other.

When I left the office that day, I was shaken. My emotions fluctuated from disbelief to frustration. I knew this wasn't about where God stood on interracial marriages. There's no such prohibition. In fact, God is all about diversity of relationships, especially culturally.

⌇

There was a hidden history behind my personal situation and the public rebuke of Bob Jones University. In 1954, the Supreme Court, in *Brown v. Board of Education*, unanimously ruled that segregation in public schools was unconstitutional. In 1964, the Civil Rights Act was passed to end segregation in universities and colleges. These were critical cornerstone legislations in the civil rights movement that exposed the reality that education and other services were not truly equal for all. Bob Jones University, by contrast, wouldn't allow Black students to enroll until 1971. When they did, they clarified there would be no interracial marriages or dating on campus, effectively continuing to enforce segregation.

To be consistent, the university had to include the Asian Americans.

I would eventually discover that decades before I came to Bob Jones, Billy Kim, a popular Korean leader who translated Billy Graham's preaching in Seoul—at the biggest meetings Graham ever spoke at—had dated and married a white woman whom he met at Bob Jones before he graduated in 1958. He had been awarded the highest student honors and was allowed to date white. Which made me wonder whether this No Interracial Dating Policy was really about Asians.

The true issue wasn't about being Asian at Bob Jones University. It was about being Black. While I had encountered racism and been bullied for my Asian-ness in Arizona, I had not experienced the deep level of racism that my Black brothers and sisters had in the South or in institutions like Bob Jones. It was bone-chilling. I was mostly oblivious to all of this history. I had been so engaged in my own teen-age struggles and fighting for myself that I lacked any type of energy or consideration to investigate more deeply how others were being hurt, abused, taken advantage of, left out, and even murdered. I was so indoctrinated and focused on my rights and the fundamentalist church's rhetoric that I missed out on the bigger challenges facing our country, such as the injustice that our Black brothers and sisters had been systemically facing for hundreds of years. When my church referred to leaders like Malcolm X or Martin Luther King Jr., they were feared not respected. I didn't know till later that historically the Church was one of the greatest perpetrators of racism, horror, and systemic oppression of the Black community, the Brown community, Asians, refugees, women, and the undocumented.

Regrettably, I didn't pay attention to the challenges faced by people of color until I found myself a victim of the same policies as my Black friends. These policies were not only discriminatory, but also absurdly inconsistent with what I knew about God. Even as I was told "no interracial dating" meant I couldn't date white women because I was Asian, if you were Hispanic/Latino, or even from the Middle East, you could date someone who looked white and was of European origins. You could be East Indian, also considered Asian, and date white. Somehow that was seen as acceptable, but physically looking Asian was not.

My situation grew worse after I made an appointment to talk to the president of Bob Jones University, Bob Jones III. The grandson of the founder possessed a winsome smile and always carried himself in a stately, well cultured manner. When I would meet him off campus, Bob Jones III remembered my name. I found him reasonable and pleasant.

I went to President Jones's large ornate office, lined with books and pictures of notable family and influential leaders in beautiful frames. It felt erudite and sophisticated, mixed with touches of family and warmth. The tall and lanky university president asked me to sit down.

"Dave, what can I do for you?"

"Well, you know there's this No Interracial Dating Policy that I got caught up in. I was wondering about your thoughts on this matter."

He responded, "Dave, God separated the races at a scene known as the Tower of Babel, implying He didn't want the races to mix. Furthermore, God told Israeli men not to marry foreign women."

I knew this was more because of their foreign gods, not because of the race. But I also knew there was no point in debating this with him. I mean, they were willing to go to the Supreme Court to fight this, as well as pay a large amount of back taxes and receive public criticism. I looked at him one more time, incredulous but trying to show him respect at the same time.

"Dr. Bob, what do you do with a situation where you have a half-Caucasian and a half-Asian person? You know my dad is white and my mom is Korean. And my brother, when he comes here, is going to be able to date white basically because he has bigger eyes than I do."

He paused, wanting to carefully craft his words.

"Dave, you have a tough situation."

He smiled and said nothing else. It seemed like he was trying to tell me he knew it was a ridiculous rule but his hands were tied with the administration. Whatever he meant, that was all he said. Interestingly, about eighteen years later, Dr. Bob Jones would go on CNN and renounce the No Interracial Dating Policy publicly.

I thanked Dr. Bob for taking the time to speak to me, but with each step I took away from him, I could feel the distance not only between us but also between me and this entire subculture of Christians that had provided answers and safety for me during a chaotic time in my life.

As an Asian, I was invisible. I became an additional victim of institutional racism first directed toward the Black community.

On some level, up to this point in my life, I think I had already accepted racism as the way things were. The political psychologist John Jost coined the term "system justification" for the findings of his studies that show that, paradoxically, people most affected by an unjust system are the least likely to question, challenge, reject, or change it. Instead, they're motivated to rationalize the status quo, not because they're happy, but because that resignation acts as an emotional painkiller. Such resignation is often taken by the majority as proof that things aren't so bad after all, that nothing needs to change. It's a vicious cycle. What I had learned growing up Asian in largely white communities was to assimilate. Don't cause trouble. In other words, hide. Just work hard. Show others you belong here by your achievement, your successes. It's what my coaches had ingrained in me in baseball and football: "Let your game do the talking." They told me to deal with dissonant truth by simply submitting to the higher authority's opinions, whether they were right or not. Don't draw attention to yourself. Stay quiet and do your work.

Many of my friends found out about my meeting with the dean and with Dr. Bob Jones III. Word of mouth spreads fast. Many came alongside me and couldn't believe what was happening. It was so incredulous to many of us. This was the 1980s, eighteen years after *Brown v. Board of Education*, establishing that racial segregation in public schools is unconstitutional even if segregated schools are of equal quality.

My dad somehow heard about the predicament I was in. We rarely talked, but this had piqued his anger enough to get him to call me on the phone. Dad worked in the justice system as a stenographer and was around the culture of lawyers and judges frequently. He could smell injustice. When Dad chose to get committed to something, he was all in. Whether it was becoming a martial artist in Shotokan karate, getting healthy, voraciously reading books, or learning how to play piano in his middle age—whenever, he was determined.

"Dave, what is this about that you can't date white? What happened?"

"Well, basically, they told me I can't date because I look Korean."

There was a long pause.

"Dave, this is ridiculous."

I could picture Dad clenching his teeth just through his tone. He did this whenever he got perturbed.

"That's unbelievable," he said again. "We need to sue them."

This felt odd coming from my father. I hadn't seen him advocate for me in this way since high school. This was the man who didn't even attend my mom's funeral.

"Dad, I can't sue them. I don't want to embarrass them or shame them publicly."

My response was based on a passage of Scripture where it says not to take your spiritual brothers and sisters to court. At the time, I didn't have the conviction to publicly address systemic injustice. It was part of my indoctrination that you just let God take care of it and respect authority even if you disagree with them. I would dramatically change my perspective about this later.

When he hung up the phone that day, it felt good that Dad wanted to fight for me.

He was actually feeling my pain and anger.

This was the dad I remembered from before the Chevy incident.

The conversation with the Dean of Men, Dr. Milton, echoed in my heart as I headed back home for the summer. The words he spoke seemed so incongruent to who I understood God to be. To discover what people actually believed—people whom I looked up to and respected—was shattering. It was a rude awakening for me. A hard but important moment to see like I never saw before. To know what people really think of you beyond the smiles and the *I love you* rhetoric was disheartening, utterly disappointing.

After those conversations, at the beginning of the summer before my junior year, I went back to Telluride, Colorado, to decide whether I was going to return to Bob Jones the following fall. There were good reasons why I should stay, but there were also plenty of reasons to leave. My mom had been tragically killed in a hit-and-run accident. I could move home to help my sister and brother adjust.

Yet my sister, Chong, was still holding on to Mom's dream that I would be the first from both sides of our family to graduate from college. Chong would step into Mom's role to challenge me not to give up.

I was leaning toward leaving BJU after these conversations with Dr. Milton and Dr. Jones. I didn't want to stay in the middle of this confusing mess where I felt unseen, an outsider. I didn't want to live under the administration always calculating my every move, especially as it related to dating their white daughters. I didn't want my social interactions scrutinized, classmates watching who I was with, reporting me to the administration. I wanted the freedom to date without any restrictions. I didn't want to be seen as this rebellious dissenter. I wanted to leave and attend university somewhere else. But this community was all that I knew. It was my world and it seemed like everything.

That summer I went back to Telluride, and on the same rock I'd experienced my first real spiritual dialogue with God as a conflicted teenager, I pleaded to God to help me figure this out. I figured He'd directly intervened with me before when I was that young teenager. Why not again? So I made my way back to that very rock in the middle of the pines. If it didn't happen, I was done. I spoke to God one more time, seeking direction.

"It's me again, God. I need your help. I don't know what to do. Should I leave the school or stay and endure the hardships because there's something there for me to learn? And by the way, I was hoping to discover my wife there. Doesn't look possible. What now?"

I opened my Bible and began to read Psalm 81, and one verse jumped out at me.

Open your mouth wide and I will fill it.

I immediately pictured an old black-and-white photograph that Mom had once showed me of me as a baby eating. Mom explained that the mess on my face and body was spaghetti and red Bolognese sauce. As I smiled at this memory, it struck me that the God I was learning about is ever present during such painful moments. The darkness amplifies God's voice. The times when it seems the odds are against you or what you are facing is impossible are when God always shows up. Could I trust God to advocate for me in ways I didn't see or understand? And more deeply, was there a purpose in my being at Bob Jones and experiencing the prejudice I faced? Perhaps I was meant to understand what my Black and brown brothers and sisters had experienced for hundreds of years before me. What is it like to knowingly live under and experience systemic injustice and oppression, especially from religious people? I had been unwilling to consider the plight of others so deeply until now.

The sky didn't open. No lightning bolts. But sitting on that boulder in Colorado, I felt a growing confidence that I would be provided for even in the midst of adversity and systemic, unjust institutional powers. I believed that somehow things would work out better than I could imagine. An optimism appeared inside me that I hadn't experienced in a while.

I knew immediately I was supposed to step back into this context of injustice. Learn from it. Know how to deal with it. I was not going to run away. If anything, I needed to understand institutional racism better. Even if that meant subjecting myself to the pain and humiliation of this educational context for another two years. I needed to experience the suffering of what others domestically had faced for centuries. I needed to understand that Koreans and other Asians had also endured generational oppression, abuse, slavery, and injustice.

On that rock in Colorado, I didn't know it, but my return to Bob Jones University would lead me to a surprising reunion. Out of the mystery would come a miracle.

CHAPTER SIXTEEN

쌍꺼풀 Sangapul— "Double Eyelids"

When I lost my mother and was told that I could no longer date white, I caught glimpses of Rebecca around the campus. I had remained friends with her but both of us had moved on to other interests.

After Mom died, the biblical character Jacob and his predicament after his mom died connected with me. A woman named Rebecca helped to ease the loss of his mom. No one replaces a loving mom, but I knew I needed the comfort of friends who were willing to be a social haven for me. Since my father's affair, the most important characteristic I cared about was someone who would be loyal. Experiencing an affair again would wreck me. I looked up the name "Rebecca" in the lexicon, and I found that her name meant "earnest devotion or loyalty."

I kept myself busy the summer after Mom passed. I focused on serving as a volunteer and working odd jobs in Arizona to make some extra spending money.

I could never have imagined that around the same time I was on that rock in Colorado, contemplating whether to return to school, Rebecca was at her home in Maryland breaking up with her basketball player boyfriend. Rebecca later told me, "Immediately after we broke up, I was thinking about my next semester classes when suddenly Dave Gibbons popped into my mind. I knew from our previous conversations that you spent a lot of time working with kids in various capacities throughout the school year and most likely during the summer that's what you'd be doing at home in Arizona." Becca paused and then said, "So I wondered how you were doing. I found myself having romantic feelings for you that I hadn't had before! I was determined to see if you were committed to someone. If not, I was going to pursue a relationship with you."

Then she said to herself, with unusual resolve, "I'm going to date Dave Gibbons."

If you know Becca, she usually doesn't speak with this much urgency and initiative. It had to be a divine intervention for me to suddenly gain this type of favor in her eyes.

Our fortuitous paths crossed at the start of the fall semester at BJU. I was now in my third year, and she was in her last year. I had arrived ready to put my head down and graduate. I was resolved to focus on my academics and to crush it with my new leadership roles in my class since I wasn't going to be able to date white women, who were the vast majority on the campus. There were a very few Asians on the campus. Not more than maybe ten out of six-thousand-plus students were Asian. So, technically I was able to date, but the point is, I wasn't able to date who I wanted to because of my race. My close friends knew what had happened to me with the No Interracial Dating Policy at the school. Soon others in the student body learned of my predicanent. I received an outpouring of sympathy but there was no uprising to defend me. I quietly resolved that finding my wife would happen later in life. This was huge for me, since the main reason I was going to university was actually to find my partner. School was a means to an end. So suddenly, I'd have to study! With Mom gone, I needed to work a couple jobs on campus to pay for my education and living expenses. Off campus I worked as a clothing and shoe salesperson in a local clothing store. I usually skipped dinner or just microwaved potatoes or popcorn in my dormitory to save money.

During the start of the school year, I was assigned to help register the whole student body for classes in the coming year, since I had worked at the men's checkout desk. It was a fun time to meet new students and also welcome back friends. One of my assigned duties was to register students whose surnames specifically began with the letter "L." I was working only a couple hours that week. A line of students started to fill the registration room where we were checking them in. In the midst of the busyness, I looked up and there she was. I was pleasantly surprised to see Rebecca Locklear standing in my line.

Sweet. I had been looking forward to catching up with her. I'm sure she thought I might be dating someone. I'd even dated a couple of her roommates. "She must be engaged," I told myself.

For her part, she told me later that she couldn't believe she was going to be interacting with me on her very first day back on campus. She had been wondering how she was going to tell me she was no longer dating that other guy. I would later discover that the moment she broke up with her boyfriend, she felt that God had divinely posited me back into her mind.

As she stood there waiting in her khaki skirt and pink polo summer shirt, her sandy brown hair flowing down to her shoulders, I had to be careful not to stare at her. *Wow, she is so beautiful.* I couldn't believe that the stars had aligned for this moment to happen. We had been assigned randomly at the same dinner table my freshmen year and now I was working at the table with the last names L–N for just a couple hours out of several days of registrations. I knew God loved me. This couldn't be just a coincidence.

"Rebecca, so good to see you!" I said when it was finally her turn in line to come speak to me. "It's been a long time." I didn't waste time or mince words. It just came out so naturally: "Are you engaged yet?"

Perhaps most guys wouldn't have been so direct, but I guess I felt this was my possible shot, my one opportunity to see if anything had changed with her relational status. I was not going to miss it. It was the subconscious flowing.

"No, we're not together anymore," she replied.

"Aww, that's too bad." I paused. "We'll have to get together and catch up sometime."

"I'd like that," Becca said with a big smile.

My heart leapt. Are you kidding? It's before my third year even starts and this is happening despite the No Interracial Dating Policy. I feigned utter disappointment, but I'm sure my voice conveyed what I truly felt—that I was empathetic but not truly sad about her predicament.

Right after she walked away, I realized spring had come. I was elated.

Becca later told me, "I couldn't believe what had just transpired."

But there was a challenge. Rebecca didn't know that my ability to date had changed on campus. When I had dated Rebecca before, I was permitted to do so. Now I was required to have someone come with us on a "date" so it didn't publicly look like a date. My poor freshman brother, Doug, new to the campus, was chosen to be the third wheel on this first date that year. It was a risk even to see her, given my new restrictions. But as long as they said I was with a group, I assumed I was safe. My interpretation of the school's rule for me was that I couldn't solo date, that I could only group date.

Doug was able to date white because he looked more white than Asian. His eyes were larger than mine, and he had the natural double eyelids, the 쌍꺼풀 sangapul. Many Koreans, like me, have a mono-eyelid—a common characteristic of many Asians. At the time, even in Korea this mono-lid wasn't popular. That's why the double-eyelid surgery became common for many Koreans. The surgery is formally called blepharoplasty. It's basically the Europeanization of the eyes.

Naturally Doug felt pity for me, and gladly came along when I was meeting Rebecca. I wrote to Rebecca to meet me at the snack shop. When she arrived and saw Doug sitting beside me, I could only imagine her questions. We hadn't spoken about race before.

After a few moments of small talk, I explained to Rebecca what was going on.

"Things have changed here at the university. I was told that I can't date white anymore."

Becca gave me a friendly smile and looked at me to say more.

"The administration says I don't meet their three-point criteria they have established to be able to date you or others that are white. I have to be culturally white, born of white or European descent, and physically look white—specifically have bigger eyes. So I can't date white anymore by myself. I'm only permitted to do 'group dates' or 'group meetups.' That's why Doug is here."

Doug gave a nervous grin and simply waved at her.

"'What do you think, Becca?"

"I'm sorry this happened to you. It's not right."

Rebecca has always had a higher sense of morality than me. She loved everything about Bob Jones University—the atmosphere, the arts, the standard of excellence, the learning and the reading, being with thousands of young adults who seemed passionate about doing good. Her private school and church, like mine, revered Bob Jones University as the best of the best. Yet when she heard what had happened to me, her perspective of the school shifted. While she appreciated the formal education, the friendships, and other aspects of Bob Jones, she also clearly saw the systemic problems and failings of schools like it. Rebecca had never considered not being with me based on the No Interracial Dating Policy. She absolutely thought the policy was wrong. She knew how her dad had been treated as someone of mixed race in the South. Because of his Native American and Black roots, he wasn't allowed to go to white schools. As a teenager at the movie theater, he would be required to sit with the non-whites up in the balcony. Becca was upset about the injustice of being mistreated simply because you looked different than others or were from a different culture.

She would later tell me the situation I was living in at the school made things clearer to her that I was the one: "The way I saw you deal with the racially charged situation caused me to respect and want to be with you even more."

The very rule that was to keep me from white women helped Becca know that I was the one for her.

We would make the best out of the awkward "group dates" that year with either Doug or with one of Becca's friends.

Eventually, I'd get called into the Dean of Men's office again. Someone had reported our dating. I was told explicitly that I needed someone to sit in between us if we got together again. Later, when other students noticed that Rebecca and I were seeing each other regularly, the administration called me into the office again and ultimately said that we had to stop the group dating. Watchful eyes were reporting us as being too "serious."

And we were. Forbidden to speak to one another, Rebecca and I resorted to writing letters every day to one another. That's all we could do. I would gently tuck her letters in their envelope to preserve the perfume she sprayed on them. Then carefully place her letters under my pillow. In our absurd, unjust situation, those notes every day were like my daily bread. Rebecca even made me this beautiful black and purple (my favorite color) blanket. It may sound a bit sentimental for a big football player but I wrapped myself in it thinking of her every day. I was in love.

After my mom died, I carried around a gaping unhealed wound. The emptiness never really goes away when you lose a loved one, but Becca's companionship and her comforting presence helped to fill the void. Rebecca made me a better person and brought a joy to my life that had been missing. It was remarkable how she just relaxed me. When I met her mom, I realized Rebecca was like her in that way. These days, I always tell Becca: "You and your mom have the best gift. When I'm with either of you, you two somehow by your very presence can put me to sleep." We laugh. The cadence and sound of their voices are so soothing. I know initially it doesn't sound like it, but that's a compliment. A restful, calming presence is their special gift.

Rebecca was born in Myrtle Beach, South Carolina. Her mother, with her very fair skin and short curly hair, reminded me of a proper Englishwoman: nose small and slightly upturned, her posture always impeccable. Being the older sister, Becca knew how to take the lead and get things done and in an orderly fashion. She would sit up straight to listen. Becca took after her mother with her femininity and love of reading, but was also like her father and grandfather, who loved building houses and riding tractors. To this day, I ask Becca to take care of the spiders in our house. It's not odd to see her lifting heavy objects, taking a chainsaw to cut down some trees, or doing what many would consider a man's job. As she enjoys pointing out, my hands look better than hers.

Rebecca's father died when she was only ten. He left behind Becca's mom, two sons, and a daughter. She is very alert to others' observations. She wasn't able to cry the day of her father's funeral because she felt everybody's eyes were on her, watching her and her brother's reactions. Her sensitivity to others' views modulates the ways she behaves or shows emotions. Becca and I may respond differently to pain, but this racial prejudice we experienced at Bob Jones united us. At that time, it felt like all eyes were on us. The university was closely monitoring our interactions. The restrictions placed on us only fueled our love for each other and surprisingly for even those who were against us.

CHAPTER SEVENTEEN

Forgiving Dad

In the still darkness of night, as I walked across a soccer field at my university, I heard God's voice in my mind.

Dave, you need to forgive your dad.

Wait. That couldn't be God. But knowing what I know about God, I knew it was unimistakably Him.

The words were as clear as the canvas of stars flickering above me. I felt without a doubt that this was God speaking to me. The words came at a random time, when I wasn't even thinking about my father. It had been a year since my mom passed away, and I wasn't even in contact with Dad. I had no desire to forgive him, so it was strange that such a strong idea would have suddenly captured my attention. I kept walking briskly across the dimly lit field, wrestling with the idea of forgiving my father.

I liked to walk around the campus at night. I had discovered that the night air cleared my head and helped me focus. The brightly colored leaves had fallen, and the frigid air had started to blow across campus. Most of the students were inside their dorm rooms or at the library studying. A few dedicated athletes were running around the track. The stadium lights were off, so there were only the streetlamps and some light from campus buildings in the distance.

Nothing about the idea of forgiving my father made sense. The pure counterintuitiveness of forgiving my dad was difficult for me to get my head around. My immediate response was a resounding "No." Forgiveness, especially if you've been wronged or are the victim of injustice, feels contrary to our instinct to fight back, or to at least demand some form of justice.

Forgiveness is a lofty idea, but this situation with my dad and his wife, Carolyn, was different. Besides, I thought I had forgiven them; I just didn't make any attempts to reconcile or stay in touch with them. I had no desire to do so. In my mind, I had forgiven him in my own way. I knew the more I thought about it, forgiveness was not just something abstractly experienced in my head. Forgiveness expresses itself in some verbal form, and even a possible physical action.

The thought of forgiving Dad in an active, physical way shook me. And frankly, it bothered me. It still didn't feel right to let the injustice go. I felt that Mom wasn't around anymore in part because of what he did. She wouldn't have been out that night and gotten killed if he'd still been with her. It was only after they'd divorced that Mom started to go to bars again. I blamed him and not Mom. I knew my mom had a choice in these matters, too, and that my dad didn't directly cause her death, but I still believed my dad was the culpable party. Not just Dad, but also Carolyn, the woman he'd had an affair with. Her role in this was even more despicable to me. It was hard for me to see her as a human.

My response to God was so immediate that I didn't hesitate to honestly say to Him:

"I have no feelings for my dad. I don't feel like forgiving him. It would be inauthentic. I'd be faking it."

An equally quick response gently returned:

Do you think Jesus felt like going to the cross?

The voice wasn't loud or angry or trying to shame me; it was a tender voice. It objectively asked me a question, like a wise sage, prompting me to process my thinking carefully. A question inviting me to wonder, to truly ask myself whether Jesus felt like dying on a cross. He wasn't giving me an answer, yet the answer became obvious through the form of a riveting question.

Ouch. I knew from what I read in Scripture that Jesus didn't want to take the path of suffering, but here I was suddenly immersed into the scene in the Garden of Gethsemane, where Jesus was sweating drops of blood because he was under such duress. Jesus prayed all night, too agonized to sleep, knowing soon he would be in the hands of angry men beating him, and nailing him to the cross. The whole gory scene went through my mind in a few seconds.

I was struck by the reality that so much of life is doing what you don't want to or feel like doing, for the sake of love. Love being transcendent over what may seem reasonable or fair or justifiable. A mother doesn't feel like waking up at 2 a.m. to feed her baby, but she does it because of love.

It's a choice to love.

My thoughts pivoted to my dad and Carolyn. Since fourth grade, I had been taught that we were to separate from those who are choosing to live in a pattern of sin or actions God clearly opposes. People from church had told me that I should part ways from my dad, because technically according to the Bible, he was living in adultery. I was encouraged to stay away from my father until he repented from his harmful choices. As for Carolyn, his new wife and coconspirator against our family, I had no desire to learn anything more about her. It was too painful even to consider her as part of us. The few times she'd called me, I abruptly stopped her, either hanging up on her or even, once, calling her an "adulteress," which is an archaic term. It sounds so extraordinarily insensitive now but that was my impulsive, angry, and self-righteous teenage self blowing off steam.

However, something in my gut said this wasn't the way of God. Separate yourself from your father to show you really love him? That didn't even make sense. This vision of Jesus agonizing in the Garden was very different from what I'd seen in the ecosystem of the religious community I grew up in. When a church or an individual separated from someone, the goal was to help that person come back to God, but it seemed Jesus did the opposite when humanity sinned. He came and dwelled among us. And stayed. Suffered and died for us.

Often Jesus chose not to separate from those others scrutinized as sinful or unclean, but drew closer to them in love in order for them to be resuscitated back to life. He reached out and touched lepers to heal them. He held the hands of the dead and brought them back to life. He protected a woman caught in the very act of intimacy with someone who was not her husband and he forgave her. He protected her from the religiously "righteous" men ready to stone her to death. And then challenged them to examine their own sins. This Jesus took forgiveness to a new level. Love would triumph over judgment. Love was chosen to supersede any law or tradition. Love in action—not a love in some abstract form in my head or love defined as separating myself from the very ones who desperately needed to experience love. All these truths taught to me since I was a child were filling my mind, breaking my heart of stone.

I paused for a moment and looked all around me. The wide and unobstructed view of the campus field I stood on reminded me of the large expanses in Arizona. I remembered our family of five arriving in Phoenix as one close and loving unit. Then I pictured my dad's blue eyes. I couldn't help but wonder what my mom thought about

Carolyn now that she was in heaven with a perfected mind. What was she thinking about this "adulteress" now?

What a random question. And what a surprising answer.

Mom would love Carolyn. And she'd want me to love Carolyn, too.

In that moment, I knew what I had to do.

Back in my dormitory room, I lay in my bunk bed. I contemplated what I felt I'd heard from God. I thought about my broken relationship with my dad and how my mom's wishes were for me to still have a relationship with my father despite how he had betrayed her. I determined that no matter how my father responded, I needed to do my part. Even though I was the younger one, the less mature one in the relationship, I had to make the move. Who was I to judge? I was guessing there was so much I didn't know between my mom and dad. Things unspoken and hidden from me that I might never understand.

I picked up the dark brown phone we had attached to the wall in our room and dialed his number. A moment later, I heard his voice on the line. He always sounded formal when he first picked up the phone.

"Hello, Gary speaking."

"Dad, it's Dave."

The pause told me he was stunned.

"Son, how are you?" You could hear the surprise in his voice.

I'm not good at small talk. So I got right to the point.

"Dad, I need to see you."

"Okay."

"And, Dad, if it's okay with you, I need to see Carolyn, too."

There was a pause.

"All right. When?"

"Can it be over Christmas break?"

"Sure."

"Okay, see you soon, Dad."

What had just happened? I took a deep breath and didn't know how it would all turn out. Yet I was confident I was doing the right thing.

I'm sure my dad was wondering what the heck was going on. Out of the blue, after months of avoiding him, I had suddenly called him. He probably assumed I was going to spew a torrent of blame, criticism, and pent-up vitriol at both of them.

When I flew home at Christmas and went to Dad's place, I resolved not to expect him to apologize. I needed to do my part to repair this fractured relationship; whatever he decided to do or not do was on him.

I took a few deep breaths in my car. Went to their condo door and rang the doorbell.

They greeted me at the door and invited me to sit down.

In the kitchen, we situated ourselves at a small table next to the wall with three chairs. Carolyn sat to my right and Dad to my left. They both looked anxious and curious. I looked at my dad and I don't know what happened, but tears started flowing instantaneously. Where were these tears coming from?

"Dad, I'm sorry. I haven't been a good son to you. Please forgive me."

Dad appeared shocked. Then I saw his face change from a protective, curious stance to one of openness and tenderness. Then I turned to Carolyn. This was the first time I had ever tried to have a conversation with her. The only time I really looked into her eyes. This was the woman my dad had had an affair with, the one who had taken the place of my mom. I was actually going to talk to her. I took another deep breath.

"Carolyn, I also want to apologize to you for how I've acted towards you. Please forgive me."

Dad wiped the tears from his eyes. His face turned red when he got emotional. Carolyn was tearing up, too, still a bit anxious as she kept nervously looking at my dad and then me.

"Son, I forgive you," Dad said, then quickly added, "And, son, will you forgive me? I'm sorry."

"Of course, Dad. I love you."

As we kept wiping the tears from our eyes, Dad stood up and hugged me. Dad had always been affectionate, so his embrace didn't surprise me. He was the one who gave big wet sloppy kisses to us kids before we went to bed. It was part of our nightly bedtime ritual as small children.

I had never expected my father to respond the way he did. But I also didn't expect all to immediately feel right. This was just the first step I had needed to take. When I embraced Dad and Carolyn, I wish I could honestly say that a flood of positive emotion overwhelmed me and that feelings of love and trust all came rushing back. They didn't.

During the whole flight back to South Carolina, I found myself gritting my teeth, still feeling disappointed in my dad, unsure whether forgiving him in such an overt way had been the right thing to do. But in the end, I felt that I had done the right thing. I guess some would call it the very act of faith. Acting in a way that you hope to be true even when you don't feel it. Hoping the actions will bear positive fruit later.

I now see the act of forgiveness like the locomotive on a train. The mindful act of forgiving someone—giving them grace for something they could never repay—comes first, like an engine on a locomotive. The feelings follow, like a caboose does after the locomotive pulls it along.

The next few years, I dedicated myself to staying in touch with my dad. I would call him, or see him in person when I could. It was a monthly rhythm. I felt I needed to lean into what was uncomfortable. For years, there were no particularly warm feelings. Yes, years.

While I was making an effort, the feelings of judgment and pain still lingered.

The emotional feeling of love eventually came. But it would still take some time for me to see Dad and Carolyn the way God sees them. It's one of those mysterious things that requires time, pain, repetition, and perspective.

Yet one thing was clearer. For much of my life my focus had been about the shape of my eyes rather than how I personally saw others with love or prejudice. The more I could see the beauty in Dad and Carolyn, the more I was able to love. The more I saw my own brokenness, the more I could love the broken. The more I forgave them, the more I could forgive myself.

CHAPTER EIGHTEEN

$1 + 1 = 3$

O n my first visit to Korea as an adult, I felt like a long-lost son finally returning home. It was the mid-1990s, and I was among a small group of Korean American leaders who had been invited to visit some of the megachurches in South Korea so we could learn from their models of growth and spirituality. At the time, eight of the ten biggest churches in the world were in South Korea. Large churches in Korea ranged from 30,000 to over 800,000 people. In Korea, whether you're Christian or Buddhist, religion is a big aspect of your life, embedded into the culture. I couldn't wait to go to see that, but I was equally excited to visit my motherland for the first time since leaving as an infant.

After getting off the plane in Seoul, I approached the immigration desk. An elderly immigration officer stood behind it, and I handed him my passport. He paused. Glanced at my eyes. Looked back down at the passport. He examined my passport and appeared confused. I knew he was wondering why I had an American passport with Gibbons as my last name yet I looked 100 percent Korean.

"한국 사람이에요?" he asked.

He noticed that I didn't understand his question, so he asked again in broken English.

"Are you Korean?"

Both his tone and his expression showed his annoyance.

"Yes," I said.

"Do you speak Korean?"

Usually I say, "I know the profanities and the food," to provoke a laugh so that I can divert attention away from the awkwardness of such a question. It would take too long to give an extended reasoning for my linguistic ineptitude. I wanted to say to him:

Sir, I'm embarrassed that I don't know the Korean language.

But I knew it didn't matter to this immigration officer. So I just said:

"No."

He briskly handed me back my passport, giving me a stern look of disgust. Then slowly and angrily punctuated each word:

"You. Should. Learn."

As I walked away from the gate, I said to myself: "Welcome to Korea, Dave."

Man, I'm not even accepted in my own country of birth.

I had expected to be fully embraced as a native Korean son coming home. This sort of rejection hurt.

Like so many others I had met in my life, this man was treating me like an outsider. Only later in life did I understand the uncertain feelings Koreans had about second-generation Asians, especially from America. Perhaps they had legitimate reasons to be dismissive of me. As a second-generation Korean American, I was considered a person of privilege. I should have become proficient in both English and Hangul/Korean. I was expected to go the extra mile because I had been given so much as an American. People like the immigration officer didn't know of my own insecurities and struggles of identity in America. They had remained in Korea and survived the great reconstruction of the homeland after the Korean War, one of the fastest economic, societal, and spiritual transformations of a nation in history. They'd struggled, too. I should have felt some of that pain, but at the time, I just saw a crotchety old Korean immigration officer. In reality, he probably just wished I cared enough to at least learn the mother tongue. Of course, modern-day Korea is much different toward those of us lost sons and daughters.

Rebecca and I married after I graduated from Bob Jones University. Rebecca had finished the year before and had completed a year of teaching English at a private school in Maryland. We were in our early twenties. We had been raised in a purity culture, which, while well intended, had significant flaws. The emphasis was on what *not* to do with potential partners, rather than what to do to have healthy relationships. I thought I was mature and ready for marriage, but really, my wife married an emotional child. I had a lack of self-awareness when it came to my own personal challenges. In fact, later, I blamed her for some of our issues: "You changed me. I wasn't this way before we got married. It's you and not me." Classic blame-shifting rebuttals of the ignorant and immature.

I had this hubris, because of my religious experience, position, and urgency to do God's work. But because you can lead in public doesn't mean you're mature in private. I created personal illusions based on external indicators more than the state of my heart.

The wounds of my past still lurked in the shadows of my soul, mostly unnoticed and under restraint. However, if I felt slighted, disrespected, or ignored, I would quickly react with anger. When I was young, I'd run away from these feelings by trying to restrain them or avoid thinking about them. As I got older, the feelings were harder to suppress.

Becca and I moved to the Mennonite and Amish farm country of Pennsylvania so I could start graduate school to obtain a master's degree in theology. But I wasn't going to be starting school right away. I had read in Jewish history that the Israeli soldier took a year off after getting married. That was a good enough reason for me not to go to grad school immediately. I wanted to spend time with my wife and do something other than study. After seventeen straight years of school, I figured it was time for a break. But what do you do with a bachelor's degree in Bible and public speaking?

That year, I landed the job of head custodian at an elementary school. It wouldn't be a job my parents would brag to their friends about, but frankly, it's probably one of the best jobs I ever had because I had so much fun working with kids. In their eyes, I was cooler than all the other adults. I loved driving the large tractor to mow the grass. Kids would look out the windows at me like I was a superhero. To the kids, I was equal to the principal. Children didn't care about titles or uniforms.

Before I got there, it had been hard for the kind elementary teachers to quiet the students. But I knew how to engage them after all those years spent working with elementary kids. In the middle of the large lunch room, bustling with the frenetic energy of kids eating lunches, I was able to quiet the kids in a couple seconds simply by raising my arm up and clenching my fist. This had always worked before. The children saw me raise my arm in the cafeteria and immediately started to quiet down, raising their arms too. It became a competition to see who could respond to me the quickest.

Teachers were in awe. They didn't know that by that time I had worked with kids for almost ten years, often hundreds of them at a time at camps or in classes. To them I was simply the blue-collar janitor, the antithesis of the Asian parents' dream of a child, one who was most likely a disappointment to his family.

Admittedly, custodial work did bring its own set of challenges. I am a germaphobe, so wiping human fluids and other things off the floors was hard. I had to clean excrement, vomit, and who knows what else regularly off walls, desks, toilets, floors, windows, and carpets. But nothing was worse than noticing how I was invisible to some teachers. I'm pretty sure they thought I must not have graduated from college because I was cleaning toilets. They had no idea that I was a university graduate going to graduate school soon. I saw how people judge you by your uniform.

Being a custodian wasn't what I had dreamed of doing when I was a kid in Maryland, but practically speaking, this custodial job was perfect for a student, so I kept it up even after I started grad school. I was allowed to study when I got my work done. Furthermore, it allowed me freedom to get acclimated to married life and to explore Pennsylvania, including the Mennonite and Amish cultures in the region. When work was done, it was done. I rarely had to think about the job after I left the campus.

Still finding my bearings after graduating from Bob Jones University, I attended a seminary known for its local church emphasis and practicality. It was not Bob Jones, but it was one small step removed. It was still a fundamentalist institution, but it felt a lot less rigid than Bob Jones. A couple of my close friends were also attending here, and learning was fun because of the people I had around me. Guys who would be friends for the rest of my life. There were four of us couples who did everything together. We were all newly married and recent graduates from Bob Jones University. The joy of this time came from our picnics, barbecues, and corn picking and husking parties. We would make creative videos and dream about the future. They were all white, and occasionally, someone said something insensitive about race, but I just laughed it off. I knew their intentions were innocent. We had built enough trust to give each other the benefit of any doubt.

School itself somehow seemed easy. Too easy. So I decided to leave and go to the graduate school where all the authors I was reading in books and commentaries were professors. I wanted to attend the renowned Dallas Theological Seminary, which offered a four-year master of theology program. I had never thought I would do more formal education, but I wanted to be prepared to be the best I could be in the pastorate.

Enrolling in Dallas Theological Seminary was considered a move away from my fundamentalist roots. In fact, my founding pastor, Dr. Simpson, who I grew up with in Arizona, wrote me a scathing letter when he found out I was going to DTS. He wrote: "I'm sorry that I taught you the things I did. You will curse the cause of fundamentalism. You have become a new evangelical [meaning I had compromised the truth I was taught as a fundamentalist Christian]. You are a liberal."

He called me the "L" word. It was like being called a "heretic." At the same time, Bob Jones University discovered I was going to DTS and wanted to get in on the fun of excommunicating me, so they sent me a letter letting me know I was kicked out of the Alumni Association. Interestingly, the letter was signed by the man who spoke at the camp in Telluride when I made a commitment to God. I felt sad for both these men, but I was convinced that there was a larger perspective of faith that I needed to explore. My time in seminary was some of the best years of my life as I gained confidence with spiritual matters and was humbled by how much I didn't know.

When I'd finished graduate school, I was hired to be on the staff of an innovative Korean church in Ellicott City, Maryland, just outside Baltimore. It was led by a bilingual first-generation Korean pastor and professor, Dr. David Sang Bok Kim. Dr. Kim was educated, well spoken, and elegant in his manner. Gentle and intelligent, he was brilliant and artful in his ability to work with opposing opinions. I had heard many stories about Korean churches where it was not uncommon for leaders to get into shouting matches or fistfights as praise and worship music was playing in the background, but there was none of that here. Heated exchanges but no physical altercations yet.

After the Bob Jones interracial dating experience, I had expected that I would be welcomed wholeheartedly at this Korean church, but while I was being interviewed for the pastoral role, I learned that there were some who didn't want me to pastor at their church because my wife was white. They thought we would be a negative role model for their children, since they wanted their children to marry Koreans. I was surprised to see how those who experience prejudice can unknowingly still perpetuate it.

The leadership of the church still decided to hire me. They would soon discover my wife was more Korean than I was! At the time, she was more sensitive and appreciative of Korean culture than I was. She felt more at home with Koreans than I did. She eagerly jumped into learning to speak Korean, became proficient in making Korean food, and ate all the Korean foods. She enjoyed wearing a hanbok, a traditional Korean clothing. Becca and I overturned some misconceptions about us, just probably not in the way they were expecting. To this day, there's only one place outside of America that Rebecca says she would feel comfortable living—the nation of Korea. It's now home for both of us.

As I began to settle into the Maryland church, it felt a little like we were living in Korea. I was embraced into a subculture that was new to me.

Living in Maryland, pastoring at the church—which to many Asians is their cultural and community social center, a home away from home—I felt genuinely happy. It was like I had hundreds of people like my mom all around me, all the time. I enjoyed it. And once the leaders who were concerned because of my American cultural personality and my white wife got to know me, they welcomed us with open arms. I saw how love could win over time.

The church was good to Becca and me. I was given a new car. It was one of the perks of being at this Korean megachurch. It was a Korean car. All the other pastors at the church had been given nice Toyotas and Buicks, but I was given a Hyundai. At the time, Hyundai was a new automaker and their quality was considered substandard. Breakdowns and mechanical failures were common. I wondered quietly why I was the only one out of our large pastoral staff to get a Hyundai. One day I mustered up the courage to ask some of my elder friends who were on the board.

"Why did you get me a Korean car when all the other pastors got American or Japanese cars?"

"Because we want to make you more Korean."

I chuckled with them, but truthfully, I had been hoping for a Toyota. At that time, they were better cars!

The others on the pastoral team also treated me like a younger brother and took care of my family; they treated my three children (at the time) like their own children. Most of them. There were always a few I could tell who were still not happy that I didn't act more Korean. But somehow in my heart I knew if I loved their children well, these uncertain and concerned feelings toward me would vanish.

The more I stepped into the cultural dynamic in the church between first- and second-generation Koreans, the more I realized I was neither. I wasn't fully part of one culture or the other. I was living in a third culture. It wasn't either/or; it was both/and. I'm not even 50 percent Korean and 50 percent American. I'm 100 percent Korean and 100 percent American. I'm $1 + 1 = 3$.

The term "third culture" is credited to American sociologist Ruth Useem, who is known for coining the term from her studies of expatriates living in India in the 1950s. "Third culture" refers to those who have a mixed identity rooted in their parents' culture of origin and the culture they themselves were raised in. While the term may have been created in the 1950s, it became popular in the 1990s, during the same time I started talking and writing about it. I had only read about the study, so I decided to apply it to myself and to my work. I concluded "third culture" was a term that could describe a growing group of globally minded citizens who knew how to adapt to any culture. While it may feel negative and debilitating at first, these third culture kids were gifted a superpower.

To me, being third culture was all about adapting. It was about having the mind-set and the will to love, learn, and serve in any culture, even in the midst of pain and discomfort.

The hard thing about being third culture is that initially you feel like you don't have a home. There is always this uneasy tension of being in limbo, an in-between state. Yet this is a gift in the long run, because you are forced to adapt. In order to thrive, you learn to function in multiple cultures and contexts. It's living in the AND. You live in the margins, yet know how to adapt into the middle of any cultural space.

I still had to learn about how third culture all worked, but I discovered that the foundation of third culture was rooted in the Scriptures that every church I knew based their vision on: love God and love your neighbor. At the time, the evangelical church was promoting church growth based on a homogeneous model—in other words, it focused on growing a church with people exactly like you. However, when I looked at Scripture, I saw that when Jesus was asked who one's neighbor was, it was the exact opposite of this. It was someone *not* like you. When Jesus was asked who a neighbor was, He shared the story about a Jew who was rescued by someone that he hated—a Samaritan. A Samaritan was half-Jew and half-Gentile, despised by the Jews. Your neighbor, according to Jesus, is someone culturally different than you. Someone you might even naturally hate.

It's not a big deal, Jesus seemed to be saying, if you love someone like you. What is miraculous and noteworthy about loving someone who loves the same things you do? The worthy ambition is when you can love someone who is *not* like you, someone you might even hate or have a tough time forgiving. Someone of a different culture, or someone you want to stay away from. The third culture person was made to love the outsider because they are an outsider. In fact, Jesus said if you can love the least of these, you've done it unto me. Jesus is the most alien among us. Our love for the outsider is like learning to love Jesus Himself.

This beautiful idea of loving the marginalized took residence in me. I knew in my soul that just because you were marginalized didn't mean you had a marginal mind or marginal gifts. Movements start in the margins. This is where Jesus is. I hungered to be in this space with other outsiders, a third culture community. I wanted to create a haven for the misfits. A place even my mom could call home.

CHAPTER NINETEEN

A Haven for Misfits

Newsong Church began in 1994 in our living room with a small group in Orange County, California. Most of the original crew was my family. I had never intended to start a church. When I was in graduate school, I told myself I would never start a new church. There were enough great churches to participate in. My plan was to take the safe path of being an associate leader, and then becoming a senior leader at one of these churches someday. Never to plant a community of faith from scratch.

But the conviction that this was the right thing to do had been growing in me as I had been seeing a generation of young Asian Americans and other people of color exit the church. Some respected Asian leaders were saying 97 percent of Asian Americans who had once gone to church were quietly exiting the church post-college. At the same time, I was seeing an ever-widening gap between the Jesus I was personally still learning about and the Jesus who had been taught to me. I was grateful for the positive gifts I'd received from many of the leaders who'd trained me, and for the ways they'd shown me the excitement of pursuing a life with God. However, I was still exploring, still trying to unravel the inconsistencies in what I had been taught. I felt an urgency and a passion to create a safe place for people who felt lost like me. I wanted to create a home for people who felt like they didn't fit in church, a place where they would feel seen, loved, affirmed, and resourced to achieve their dreams. A place where questions were welcomed. A place where their pain could be shared and eventually turned into a superpower.

What kept this front and center for me was the deep scars of remembering how Mom didn't fit in the church. I thought about this all the time. I was motivating myself to turn her pain into a purpose. To let my pain become a platform to empower people like Mom. My pain would become a gift to connect me to others who maybe wouldn't relate to my successes, but would certainty relate to my suffering and confusion. Eventually, this pain would guide me to passionately care about people like my mom, who needed a community who would love her just as she was.

I thought that through Newsong, maybe I could create not only a home for me and my family, but a place where those like my mom could be at home. It would be a place for both young and old. Koreans and Americans. Black and brown. Poor and rich. Love would guide us more than laws. It would be more about the spirit of the law versus just the law itself.

Rebecca was pregnant with our fourth child, Megan, and the three others were preschool or kindergarten age when we moved to California to start the church. We launched with small beginnings, mostly Becca, my kids, and a couple of friends who believed in this vision.

Then Newsong took off numerically. We became one of the fastest-growing churches in America. At one point, Newsong was one of the largest second-generation Asian American churches in America. Over the years, we would meet at a variety of places—multiple hotels, a football field, a conference room, a park, an Elks Lodge, and even a nightclub. We continued to grow as many next-generation Asians started to hear about this new place for misfits like them.

Internally, I had second thoughts about starting this church as soon as we arrived in California. But I believed in my vision and had a strategic master plan to go with it. A vision to start a movement where the hub church would be in Orange County, but would help launch spiritual communities all over the world. I could feel the beginnings of what I saw in the Black church with the Asian church in America. There would be Asian Americans and an emerging third-culture people influenced by the church (positively and negatively) who would become the next generation of creatives, innovators, and entrepreneurs. Their church experience, if like an X-Men academy, could launch them into their dreams.

My pre-launch plan was to seek the blessing from some of the well-known influential churches in Seoul, South Korea, and in the United States. I didn't want Newsong to be seen as rebelling or antagonistic toward our homeland or the ethnic churches that already existed, but honoring and appreciative of our elders' sacrifices. I remember reading this quote from someone unknown: *He who forgets the past is not fit to be a pioneer.* It's similar to the well-known statement from George Santayana, a Spanish-born American philosopher and one of the most important thinkers of the first half of the twentieth century, who said: *Those who forget the past are condemned to repeat it.*

The support came in not only from well-known Korean pastors like Pastor Hah Young Jo from Onnuri Church but also others. A set of mostly first-generation Korean parents from my home church in Maryland banded together to promise me monthly support to work on this vision. They collectively donated every month to help with our dream. When I arrived in Southern California, one of our biggest supporters and answers to prayer was Bob Shank, the lead pastor of South Coast Church, which is now called Mariners Church. South Coast was a nondenominational megachurch congregation in Irvine with thousands of churchgoers, but very few members of the Asian population. Bob Shank offered to partner with me and share their resources with us.

"Dave, I can't give you any money, but I can give you something better than money," Bob told me. At the time, I didn't know what could be better than money. When I asked what that was, Bob told me to go home and pray about it, then come back to him with a list. So I did as he suggested. When we met again, I knew what to ask for.

"What if we had a place to meet at your church on Sunday mornings?" (Mornings are prime time for churches.)

That wasn't the only thing I asked for. I also asked if we could have offices at his church and if we could interact with and be led by his all-star staff. Then I asked whether we could have the kids from our community blend into the children's programs of their church, because we wouldn't have a lot of people ready to serve. My wife looked at the list and said, "Dave, that's a lot. Don't ask for so much."

With fear and trepidation, I gave him my list of about ten bold requests.

Bob quickly scanned each request, looked up, and surprisingly said, "No problem, Dave."

When Newsong held its first service in a small conference-size meeting room at South Coast Church, we had close to a hundred people gathered together to worship. The majority were young Asian adults, mostly Koreans and Chinese Americans. We quickly filled the room they gave us to meet in. As we grew, they kept opening up bigger rooms for us and moving their mostly white congregants from those rooms into other spaces. And they allowed us to meet during prime time on Sunday mornings, not some random time in the afternoon when most people wanted to be outside in the large playground we know to be Southern California. Where else in the world can you both snow ski and surf on the same day?

We were on our way to creating this home for the misfits, and largely because a generous group of mostly white Christians treated us like family.

A decade later, I found myself in the packed Anaheim Convention Center, right next to Disneyland, with thousands physically streaming into our service. It was Easter of 2004. I stood watching the worship band playing and the choir singing. Electric guitars wailed and drums pounded through the space. Lights bounced off the stage while piped-in smoke drifted over the surface. It felt like being at a rock concert.

The crowd of mostly twenty-somethings stood watching this spectacle. As I stared out over them, waiting to deliver my Easter message, I couldn't help thinking how mammoth and surreal this gathering looked. This was almost every pastor's secret dream, but I realized that I didn't know if it was mine.

What am I doing?

These unspoken feelings had been growing within me for a while. Now more than ever, I couldn't let them go. Like the rising volume of the music, the tension continued to intensify. I knew God was in this place, but watching it all now, I wondered if this was how He wanted us to use the gifts and resources people had sacrificed. This service felt more like a Disney fireworks show than a worship experience.

Newsong was in the midst of fund-raising for new property that could adequately accommodate our growing numbers of mostly young adults and families. We had built this dynamic community for ten years, climbing and inspiring our people to go for it. It was always about the "next level." We had laid everything all out on the line. I tried to soak it all in. This was like getting to the top of Mount Everest, from a professional perspective. This was what success had looked like to me when I'd first envisioned a church.

The dream for Newsong had been to convene diverse, misfit people together to listen and to understand each other's story and to provide access to quality resources from our flourishing community. And for the first ten years, we did bring people together. With an enviable average age of twenty-eight, we were unique in the diversity of young people, mostly Asians at the time, who were coming.

That first decade was a blur. We were all hustling. From the outside perspective, we had this meteoric rise. We were off the charts in the classic metrics of growth. But a weariness was setting in. I felt that we were growing larger, but not deeper. The more I thought about this, the more unsettled I became. There was this growing anxiety that maybe I was climbing the prescribed ladder of success only to realize the ladder was leaning against the wrong wall. Because of our numerical size we looked successful, but gathering a large crowd doesn't mean success. A large crowd can just be a spectacle. A fireworks show with a lot of colorful lights, sounds, and designs, but few enduring transformational qualities.

I had a growing sense that I was perpetuating an illusion of success but no deep change was taking place. Perhaps we were big vertically, but we weren't expansive in helping people live out a healthy life outside the four walls of our church.

Perhaps globally we were faring better. We launched economic incubators like fish farms in Thailand, and we even built schools for children who didn't have access to quality education. Yet locally our focus was mostly internal programs. I started reading verses in the Bible about how God isn't impressed with our singing and prayers. That real worship is loving the widows and the orphans. And in another passage, I read:

He has shown you, O man, what is good;
And what does the LORD require of you
But to do justly,
To love mercy,
And to walk humbly with your God? (Micah 6:8 NKJV)

I don't think I was doing this type of merciful work effectively. I concluded that to be a person of justice was to do the hard work of love. Doing the work was more than an inspiring talk or one special Sunday focus.

Just before I stepped out to deliver my message to those thousands that Easter morning, the crowd that had gathered was caught up in the energy of all the people and in the show produced that day. I had the Michael Jackson wireless microphone meticulously taped to my ear and wrapped around the back of my head when I heard a voice.

Is this it?

I didn't know where the voice came from, whether it was God's voice or mine. But yeah, *is this it?* Is this what I had envisioned as success when I thought about serving God while I was in high school?

Earlier, the church had discovered a large stretch of land for sale off Interstate 5 in Orange County. During the campaign to raise money for our new home, the mantra I had been using was, *It's not about the building; it's about what happens inside the building.* I had purchased a pastor's financial campaign kit that shared this hack to help you to raise capital for a building initiative.

We ended up raising millions of dollars. But something still felt off inside me. I should have been more excited. When we put in a bid to the local real estate developer in Irvine, California, we had eight campuses globally (Paris, Mexico City, Bangkok, Los Angeles, Fullerton, Irvine, Pasadena, and Dallas) and helped with two other successful church launches, but this building would be the main hub or the global headquarters. We were ready to build a premier destination site for all to see. The land was just off Interstate 5, which runs not only through Southern California, but all the way up the West Coast. Hundreds of thousands of cars would pass our future site every day. This would be the crown jewel especially for Korean Americans and other Asian Americans when it came to church. It was only fitting to have the church in one of the most publicly visible locations in Southern California.

But then we got a call. The real estate developer said, "You can't buy the land."

I said, "Why not?"

It turned out Kia Motors Corporation was allegedly offering $1 million more than we could offer. My own Korean brothers and sisters! We had to let the property go. And with it, I had to let go of the dream. I had no idea how I could keep growing the church without this large physical hub.

I went into a funk. Now we had been denied the opportunity for a new building. I wasn't sure what to do next.

Grieving the loss and all the effort in trying to acquire this land, I think I heard God's voice this time.

Why are you so disappointed, Dave? Didn't you say it's not about the building but what happens inside the building?

The next question God asked convicted me even more:

Isn't what happens outside the building more important than what happens inside the building?

The reason this question messed with me so much was because I couldn't honestly answer it.

In a gentle and simple manner, I heard God answer this question with another.

Dave, what would the church look like if it weren't confined to a piece of land?

It was like God was speaking Martian to me. I had no idea what He was talking about. I had been trained to build the church on a huge property so we could continue growing. What now? We had campuses in the United States and globally, but it still didn't seem enough. This constant quest for growth and numbers was like *Groundhog Day*, or a song playing on an infinite loop. The adding of sites and services could go on forever. I eventually told my staff I didn't want to be a pastor anymore. It got so bad, I started saying the same thing during Sunday messages: "I don't want to be a pastor. The only reason I'm doing this is out of obedience." My heart wasn't in it. But the people kept coming. It was odd—it didn't matter what I said, the church kept growing. They said, "Man, Dave is so authentic." But I felt like I was authentically dying.

It would take some cows and a City of Angels to speak to me.

CHAPTER TWENTY

Beyond the Uniform

D ave, I think you'd be a great commodities trader. You like risk.
You have a global perspective. You can process data and you're
not afraid to make a call. We can make a good amount of money and
give it away to causes we believe in. You want to give it a shot?"

I almost couldn't believe what I was hearing from Paul, a friend
of mine. He was one of the first Asian American commodity traders at the Chicago Board of Trade, and now he was inviting me to
start a futures trading company with him and a couple other novice
investors.

"I'll help you out and give you the capital you need to start investing," Paul said. "What I have is yours. We're brothers. You can trade
my money." Who says stuff like that to you? It seemed like little risk
on my part. The upside was huge.

How could I refuse such an offer?

The next several years became a blur. I dove into the investing waters while remaining involved with the church. Paul and two other friends, Mike and Henry, would show up at the office around 5 a.m. to start our day, and we would end around 1:30 p.m., the time the markets closed, and I went to the church after this. We set up the offices in Newport Beach near the Pacific Ocean, at the famous Fashion Island Outdoor Mall. I learned to trade everything from corn, soybeans, wheat, and even pigs and our favorite cattle to silver, gold, and palladium.

Henry always made sure we got good food, like breakfast burritos, or if we felt like we had to be healthy, vegetable and fruit smoothies. Mike, Paul, and I would listen to the news happening around the world. A political coup or the taking down of a corrupt political leader could cause markets to shift. Paul would also call the weather services we paid for that gave us forecasts of daily, weekly, monthly, and potential drought conditions, storms, flooding. Then we rounded it out by calling the grain farmers and, of course, our favorite guys—the cattle farmers.

I never gambled, but that was what this felt like to me. The difference between gambling and trading, Paul assured us, was we were making decisions based upon data and taking educated, calculated risks. The highs were incredible and the lows were like someone "kicking you in the balls," as Paul would say. If you've ever been in a losing trade, where you're hemmorhaging massive amounts of money, you know what this pain feels like.

We were a few months into our learning curve of trading when we began to believe that cattle prices were headed lower. So we did what we called a short trade. We kept adding to the position that said the cattle markets were going to weaken. However, the market thought otherwise. We got to the point, after building a rather large position, that we had margin calls. This meant that the brokerage house was saying that we were over-leveraged and now owed them money if we wanted to keep our positions.

Paul looked at me with his serious and sad eyes and said, "Sorry, Davey, we're going to have to roll out of our position and take the loss." For some reason, we added "ie" or "y" to each other's names at random times. It was evidence of our affection for each other.

"Paulie, I think one more day is important. Can we hold on to this position at least one more day?"

I didn't want to tell him I had prayed about it and felt some confidence in our position, because if you're a serious investor, you don't want to blame God for the loss if you make a bad decision. Also, it looks unprofessional, like you're not doing your homework and relying more upon chance. Does God really care about our profit and gains? Bottom line, Paul warned us that we could pray, but just don't tell anybody.

"Okay, we can wait one more day," Paul said. Later that day, we were together and saw a breaking news report on the television screens.

"Mad cow disease has been reported among cattle in the United States," said a television reporter.

As soon as we heard that, our hearts sank.

Oh no—it's going to affect our position. We're going to get crushed!

In commodity trading, you have the potential to lose more than you invest. We looked to Paul, who was gravely concerned as well. He would typically invest multiple times what the rest of us would trade, but in this trade we were all heavily vested in our "short" position with cattle.

Paul had weathered many ups and downs as a trader. He calmed us down and said:

"Guys, let me make sure we're in the wrong position. I'll call the cattle rancher we talk to regularly."

We all stood looking at Paul then one another, nervously awaiting the cattle rancher to answer Paul's call.

It didn't look good because, in our minds, if cattle were scarce, that would drive up the prices. As Paul made the call, we waited with bated breath. Paul asked the cattle rancher, "Well, are prices going down or up since there's mad cow disease reported in America?" Then he smiled and said, "Guys, the markets are going down! We're on the right side of this trade." We started celebrating.

We'd made a historic trade that was noted by global financial news. We were called the "Asian cowboys."

Making that windfall early on made us feel invincible, which was not good.

At this same time, the church kept growing despite my reservations about my role at Newsong and whether I should even be a pastor. I was confident that God wanted me to be free from the church. Our success at trading seemed like an indication of God's affirmation of us.

However, God had something else in mind. We rode the success of that trade for a while. With our next big trade, I told God that if we failed, it would be a sign that I was not supposed to be in this type of business as a trader. The work itself and being with the boys every morning, launching and making fun of each other, was a dream but exhausting. As with the mad cow trade, we were on margin call for a soybean trade. Like before, I asked Paul to wait one more day because I was convinced we had the right trade position. He did, but the market kept going against us. With sadness, Paul looked at me and said, "Sorry, Davey, we have to get out of our position and take the loss."

As soon as I called the trading house and rolled out of my position, the markets immediately went in the direction of our original position.

The fellas in the office started laughing. They had known I was all in on this trade.

It was clear I had to move on.

Feeling like a failure and with no extra capital that could lead me into my next career, I resigned myself to seeking out God's plan for my life. I was in disbelief it wasn't commodity trading. Why would God take me out of something that was so fun and lucrative? We were giving so much money away.

That's when Paul pulled me aside and said something I'll never forget:

"Dave, we can find other great traders to invest. But there aren't too many people that can lead others spiritually like you can."

I didn't want to hear that. But I knew I needed to step away from trading. To reboot. I needed to reexamine my life. I told the leadership at Newsong I needed a sabbatical. My family and I decided to go to Thailand for a year. My hope was that I would gain clarity about what was next for me and my family. My guess was that church wasn't a part of the answer, and I needed some space to think of other directions. Why Thailand? When I visited the work that our church supported there, I felt a connection to the Thai people. It felt like home, and it felt like the Narnia of my childhood. The spiritual energy of Thailand was off the charts.

I was introduced to a pioneer in community development work in Northeast Thailand by the name of Jim Gustafson. Jim was white physically but was Thai culturally. His smile and laugh were contagious. He moved with freedom and speed. He spoke fluently in both Thai and English. Jim had a vigor and youthfulness about him that was attractive. As he got older, he seemed positively younger. He was in his sixties at this time. You could tell he was made for Thailand. He absolutely loved the country and its people. I rarely meet someone like him filled with so much authentic passion and love. He had a PhD in agriculture and also an advanced degree in theology. He did groundbreaking work when it came to integrating spirituality and economic/social development, especially with those who were considered the outcasts of a culture. When I traveled through Bangkok and then the rural regions of Thailand, I felt the deep spirituality of the nation and the vibrant energy pulsating within the people. I've traveled extensively and it's hard to find a friendlier country that welcomes the foreigner. It's a growing international hub for art, food, design, and health tourism.

It was about the same time I was doing the commodity trading that the great tsunami of 2004 in Southeast Asia took place and devastated portions of Thailand. Over 5,000 people died in Thailand, and in Indonesia over 240,000 people were killed. The world was horrified. My eyes and heart were drawn to Thailand. I knew when my trading days were over that this was where I was supposed to go for my sabbatical. I asked Rebecca and my four children what they thought. Surprisingly, they were all for it.

The original City of Angels is not Los Angeles. This city has a long name that is rooted in Pali and Sanskrit:

Krung Thep Mahanakhon Amon Rattanakosin Mahinthara Ayuthaya Mahadilok Phop Noppharat Ratchathani Burirom Udomratchaniwet Mahasathan Amon Piman Awatan Sathit Sakkathattiya Witsanukam Prasi.

The shorter name is: Krung Thep Maha Nakhon, meaning the Great City of Angels. You know it as Bangkok.

After the tsunami, Newsong and the local indigenous Thai organization we partnered with had gained credibility with the Thai government and other NGOs because we helped to build schools and launch businesses for economic development. Our church also started a marine research development organization to help fishermen to farm the most profitable fish in the Andaman Sea and helped start fish farms to support the local economy so that young people wouldn't sell their bodies to care for their families.

⌒

I remember the wonder I felt about living in Greensboro, Maryland, when I was a kid. Arriving in Bangkok felt like walking into Narnia. It was like a real *Jungle Book*. We could feel the pulsating life of the city as soon as we landed. At the time, Thailand had 65 million people, and Bangkok had around 13 million inhabitants, about 1 million of whom were expats or internationals. Bangkok is commonly stereotyped as a destination for sex tourism. But the country is also known as the land of smiles, fittingly, because the kindness of the people is magical. Thailand is known for her hospitality. Our family loved everything about our time in Thailand.

Every day, five minutes into our usual walk through one of the nicest areas of Bangkok, we would hold our breath for five seconds because of the open sewer we were passing. At first, we were shocked by the pungent odors. The smell was so strong, it seemed like the odor became embedded in our clothes. Yet over time the smells of the city grow on you—the fragrant flowers, the street food frying, baristas making fruit juices and coffee. The mixture of the good and not-so-fragrant smells became the very thing we loved about Bangkok. By the end of our first year there, we'd still hold our breath as we passed the sewer, but then we'd just look at one another and burst out laughing, letting the odor clear our nostrils and breathing more deeply once we were past it. There was a fullness of experiencing it all together.

While we were in Bangkok, life slowed down. In Southern California, it's not uncommon for people to spend three or even six hours every day in their car alone with the windows up, speeding along the freeway at 80 miles an hour or sitting in traffic hating everything. In Bangkok, we got around by walking. We learned how to catch currents and openings in the crowd to flow with locals and internationals. Immersing yourself in the streets allows you to see things you don't notice at high speeds. You hear laughter and snatches of conversation, and stop to sample the wide array of colorful food and desserts sold by the street vendors. In Bangkok, I rarely felt alone.

The gift of living in Bangkok was the joy I found again there. It was a joy that I had lost in the hustle of life. I had been working so intensely that I was missing out on my kids growing up and the wonderful, diverse community that was blossoming around me. When you're driven and have FOMO, you get more compulsive and exhausted. It's easy to mistake adrenaline for positive energy until it all comes crashing down around you. Overuse of adrenal glands is toxic.

Why had I been hustling so much, trying to force the game? I think my life had become all about trying to prove who I am. I was so used to being the odd man out whenever I entered a space that I worked extremely hard to prove I belonged.

Bangkok awakened me. The beauty and magic of the OG City of Angels brought me to seeing with childlike eyes once again. All this happened as I began to get to know a few people who were very different from me.

We had moved to Thailand with high hopes and high spiritual aspirations. We planned to start a church there, and we saw how quickly people were interested in the way we did church. So we started meeting in our twenty-fourth-floor apartment overlooking the financial district of Bangkok. Shoes lined the hallway outside our door. Our home was filled literally wall-to-wall with people. When we rented space at a popular nightclub where Westerners came to party, the crowds flooded in.

A man named Boyd Kosiyabong came to one of our gatherings after hearing that there were some odd people from America starting a church in the nightclub district of Bangkok. When I first met Boyd, I saw a humble man wearing a light blue polo shirt and shorts.

He was a former Buddhist who was exploring Christianity. He was fascinated that we weren't "religious" in the way he'd come to expect from Christians. We would wear shorts and flip-flops. Occasionally our team would talk too loud or accidentally show the soles of their feet or cross their legs, unknowingly pointing at someone with their feet. To Thais, showing the bottoms of your feet to someone was like saying F you. There was much we did to offend people yet somehow there were key people like Boyd who were so spiritually hungry, they were able to see past our naïve culturally taboo offenses. Boyd wanted to meet me. I was surprised when he asked if I would help him grow spiritually and help give him some ideas of what to do with his then struggling business.

We discovered Boyd was one of the most famous popular composers in Southeast Asia. After he invited me over to his home to meet his wife and two children, I saw that Boyd felt things deeply and gave himself completely to care for other people. He composed music about the heart and love. People would cry while singing his songs. They were ballads that would make you feel like you were home.

In business, the bottom line is profit, the dollars earned or the customers acquired and retained. For churches, the number of attendees during a given weekend is often the key metric of success. Boyd taught me that the most important metric may be one person. He'd mentor young musicians, helping them form unique bands, giving them access to the best resources. Boyd himself could impact the whole nation in one day. He had 80 percent brand recognition in Thailand. That meant that of the 65 million people in Thailand, about 52 million people knew Boyd. He was a marketer's dream. Boyd showed me how important it is to love one person well. One person could change a city. One person could change a nation. One person could change the world.

Previously, I had stretched myself thin as I worked frantically striving to build this dream community. There might be thousands of people in the audience at Newsong, but it was hard to focus on one of them. When I was on a big stage, I was just talking into blinding lights. The audience became a blur to me. Like one big mass of humanity. As I worked with Boyd, I started asking myself, what if I'm called to work with just one person? What would it look like to inspire and love people like Boyd, who needed customized development with their unique array of gifts and challenges? Previously, I'd felt I had to be in front, because that's what leaders seemed to do. But when I got to know Boyd, I saw I didn't have to be in front. I could love and support Boyd, helping him to reach his dreams, and he would have a greater impact on people than I ever could by myself. Basically, if I was willing to be second and focus on serving others, I could be engaged in more meaningful and impactful work. And I wouldn't have to work as hard. In fact, more actual good work would be accomplished. Since I am an introvert, this vision for my life was contrary to the metrics of success I had focused upon since I started my journey as a pastor.

In our time together, Boyd refocused on his health and family. From there, he was able to adapt his businesses to thrive. He ended up letting go of one company, which let him focus on what he really cared about: resourcing young people to be able to make a living and support their families with their music.

Although Boyd had initially come to me for guidance, there was so much that he taught me. By the time I went to Bangkok, I had become disillusioned with the American church empire building as I knew it. There were aspects of it that felt very consumeristic and driven by a pace that was unhealthy. American churches were focused on maximum growth among people who were similar. It was all about making people feel comfortable and focusing on people just like you.

But a question kept coming up in my mind: What should people feel uncomfortable about? Jesus walked the road of suffering. He became human flesh, was ridiculed, beaten, falsely accused, betrayed, and crucified. It seems God's way is often about suffering that leads to life.

That reminded me of the original vision of Newsong. We existed to love the outsiders. Those who had been marginalized. Discarded. Left to survive on their own. The darkest and hardest places were to be the places we chose to go.

Then I started thinking about who are the ones that need love today but are often rejected or hurt by the church. People like my mom, who never felt at home. Those were the people I wanted to focus on. And people like Marina, who was once houseless, living in a van with her partner, who had suddenly been thrust into global fame.

⌒

Marina is considered the Grandmother of Performance Arts. She is revered by artists, entertainers, the billionaires club in Silicon Valley, and young people all over the world. Her name is Marina Abramović. My children told me that every serious artist knows who Marina Abramović is. I wasn't a serious artist, so I needed to read up on her because my fashion friend from Mexico City was opening a shop in New York City. She had this strong sense I was supposed to meet her.

I discovered that Marina was a legend in the arts world.

The exhibit that put her on the map was called *The Artist Is Present*. It was held at the Museum of Modern Art (MoMA) in New York City. People waited hours in line just to look Marina in the eyes. Marina shared: "Nobody could imagine...that anybody would take time to sit and just engage in mutual gaze with me." In fact, the chair was always occupied, and there were continuous lines of people waiting to sit in it. The MoMA website noted, "It was [a]complete surprise...this enormous need of humans to actually have contact."

Beginning in the early 1970s, Marina was experimenting with the complex relationship between the artist and the audience. She tested the limits of the audience and herself, physically, emotionally, intellectually, and spiritually. Because of the nudity, blood, and symbolism she uses in her performances, some in the Christian world labeled her demonic or a worshipper of Satan.

This raised my curiosity, not my concern.

I had been going to New York City every month to advise a global fund investor as part of the consulting work I was doing more and more, so I looked at the dates and they matched the grand opening of my fashion friend's store.

Mercer Kitchen was this cool, comfortable place in SoHo where my designer friend was going to celebrate her Grand Opening Party. I arrived and most of the people were already there. I sat as, again, I'm not quite comfortable with cocktail talk normally. As I waited, there was suddenly a hush that prevailed in the room. People started staring at the main entrance to the room. Some were obvious. Others were more discreet with their quick glances, acting like they really didn't care but did. I rose to go and greet her. She had several assistants to help her. Marina was in her mid-sixties at the time but still looked young. She had long dark hair. Piercing eyes that were curious and knowing at the same time. Confident yet you could tell she, too, battled with the demands of the crowds. Being an artist who needs to sell product, you have to be out and about connecting. It's exhausting work. It's part of marketing your brand, your products, and your art. It's expected by the galleries you are committed to or your own company to be networking among possible patrons.

I stood calmly next to the fashion designer from Mexico who had invited me to meet Marina. She had felt we needed to meet. The designer welcomed Marina with customary kisses on the cheek and gratitude for her coming. And then my friend said, "Marina, I want you to meet Dave." Marina looked at me. Smiled, paused. And then gazed into my eyes, asking, "What is your energy?"

"Oh, it's an energy that is above all other energies."

She responded quickly, "You must sit by me. Is that okay?"

We sat next to each other and I could sense who she was beyond her performances and beyond what I know some Christians would say. She was a deep person, spiritually astute, and a seeker of truth and love. She would do anything to taste and see something that couldn't be satisfied in this world. This whole download of who she was happened in seconds. I felt I knew her.

In a few moments, she then turned to me and said, "Dave, I think you can help me. Will you be my spiritual adviser? And I think you could also help my company turn around? Can you come by my office tomorrow and meet my team?"

"Of course! I'd love to."

What had just happened? As I sat there, excited about the possibility of working with Marina and walking with her on her spiritual journey, I remember whispering to God in my heart, *How do I help her? You know I'm new to this type of interaction outside the Christian bubble.*

My whole life was about trying to get people saved. This transactional perspective put me in awkward situations where I felt more like a salesman hyping a product or a multilevel marketer doing a bait and switch. It was so odd and inauthentic to me.

Find out what her dreams are and help her fulfill them.

Wow. So oddly simple yet profound. This was something that I could imagine Jesus saying. It was the opposite of the way I had been trained. It was usually about being nice to somebody and bringing them to church. Then eventually having them join our vision for how we can change the city and the world. But this approach with Marina was all about love. It was about her dreams, not mine.

Months later, Marina and I were praying together. She had held her hands, praying every word with sincerity and urgency. After the prayer, Marina exclaimed, "I've never felt an energy like that before." I said, "Yes, there's no one like Jesus." He is the energy above all other energies.

This encounter and my relationship with Marina over the next few years changed me probably more than it changed her. I now saw that the work I was called to do was beyond a uniform or occupational title of pastor or trader or senior adviser. I was called to be a lover and one who authentically serves people. There was no need for me to be point or lead. I needed to be myself. An introvert who, if necessary, could be an extrovert. But no need to sell, or be what some call a "hypepriest."

All through my life, I realized it was other people who had helped me see who I was, from my mom and sister to my close friendships and now Marina Abramović. My life was beyond Sunday. It was beyond a job title. Jobs are like uniforms or fashion that can help express who we are, but the clothing doesn't make us. Fashion changes. Jobs change. What I now realized was that the uniform I wear is not my identity. My identity was around something more transcendent, purposeful, significant, and spiritual but not religious. I was called to love others without any ulterior motives or strings attached.

CHAPTER TWENTY-ONE

One Last Kiss

While I was still living in Bangkok, I got a call that shook me.

"Dave, it's Dad. I'm in the hospital."

He didn't sound well. His strong voice, usually brimming with confidence, was noticeably weaker, worn by hardships and choices that he regretted. He paused for a long time, catching his breath, even as he tried to sound normal.

"What's wrong, Dad?"

"Son, I got leukemia."

My father had just turned sixty-five. This was the moment he had been waiting for—he was excited about finally retiring. But now, just when it was his time, he was diagnosed with leukemia.

I felt something grip my heart as I stopped breathing for a moment, trying to fathom what was happening. At this point in our relationship, the past wounds were healing. There was a scar, but no more stinging or pain. The memories of the hurt remained, but I couldn't feel the pain anymore. I was even connecting with his wife, Carolyn, regularly. She had started treating me like her own son, sometimes even better. I know my mom would have been shocked by how far we'd come. She would have been delighted that my relationship with my father was restored.

I sprang into action mode and created a plan.

"Dad, I'll fly back home. I'll stop in California for a moment to see the staff I work with but then hop on over to Arizona to see you in the hospital. I have a close friend named Larry Kwak, who works at MD Anderson. I'll give him a call. He's a specialist in lymphoma. But he has connections. He's like a brother to me. He's one of *Time* magazine's '100 Most Influential People.' I know he can help us."

"All right, son. Love you, Dave."

"Hey, Dad, we got this. I'll be there soon. I love you, Dad."

On my long flight across the Pacific Ocean, moving from the humid heat of Bangkok to the dry heat of Phoenix, I wondered if my dad was feeling regret. Retirement was within reach, and now he might die the year his retirement was going to kick in.

He and Carolyn had accumulated a couple of houses, a condo in Northern Phoenix, and a beautiful cabin in Strawberry, Arizona. They'd made some modest investments that were paying off. My dad had learned how to save, probably from my mom. He was frugal and never extravagant. His early years living in poverty made him careful with his expenditures. His only real personal splurging was with new cars. He had always loved his cars.

About twenty hours later, I landed in Phoenix, got my rental car, and hustled to the hospital. When I saw Dad, he looked despondent, underneath the white sheets, IV bottle hanging near him on a long pole. He'd already resigned himself to the fact that he might die soon, especially if his body didn't respond to the radiation and chemo treatments.

I approached him with a smile, standing close to him as he sat up in his bed. I tried to be as positive as I could, hoping that the retirement he'd dreamed of was still possible for him.

"Hey, Dad, we can beat this thing. Don't give up. I'm sure my friend can help us. He's been a friend for a long time. I already talked to him and he's checking on some possible treatment options and doctors that can treat your leukemia. He used to be considered a quack with his immunotherapy experiments, but now he's considered to be at the forefront of cancer research. People are actually getting healed of their cancer. He's one of those guys that may win a Nobel Prize someday."

"That's great, son."

Larry came through for us. Larry got my dad into one of the treatment programs at MD Anderson in Houston, a world-renowned cancer treatment center. Dad would have some of the leading physicians in the world caring for him. Dad and Carolyn started making regular trips to Houston, and Dad's health improved dramatically. We were all hopeful. After he had a bone marrow transplant, we continued to see success. He was going to beat this thing.

Then I got a surprising call from Dad after several months of positive news.

"Dave, I'm going to stop going to Houston."

"What? Why? Dad—you're getting better. The treatment is working."

"Carolyn doesn't want to keep making trips to Houston," he said as his voice grew quieter. "It's hard for her."

Hard for her? *Are you serious?* I said to myself.

She must have been near him listening to the conversation. This didn't make sense, so I tried to talk some reason into him. I was thinking that was awfully selfish of Carolyn.

"Dad—it's up to you. The plan is working. You can't just stop after you've gotten this far."

"I know, but it's just too much for Carolyn. She wants to be home. I can continue some treatment at the Mayo Clinic near me...In fact, it's what *we* want."

I didn't believe it. Dad wouldn't want this. He just didn't want Carolyn to feel uncomfortable.

I was upset with Carolyn.

I did all I could to hold back from saying how ridiculously selfish Carolyn sounded. All the negative feelings I'd had for her began to resurface. She started to complain about the cost of the hospital. It seemed her comfort and cost were the main issues, not Dad's health.

This news was hard on my siblings, too. My brother, Doug, was Dad's best friend. Dad and Doug shared a relationship that seemed more like brothers than father and son. They could just look at each other and read each other's mind. I always felt good for Doug that he had this closeness. Doug was also most like Dad in personality. More serious, but a great sense of humor. Focused and determined. Doug was good-looking, tall, and athletic. Doug and Dad had taken up karate together and would often playfully practice moves whenever they were next to each other—in the car, the house, or outdoors as we were walking together. I know this decision prompted by Carolyn was especially hard on Doug. This would be extremely challenging for him when it came to his relationship with her.

Dad continued treatments at the local Mayo Clinic in Phoenix instead of going to Houston. He started to get worse. We naturally blamed Carolyn. She felt it, because she wasn't able to look at us. She also was now dealing with the potential loss of her confidant and best friend. Dad was her security. She didn't hang out with too many others, not even her own siblings and son from her first marriage. When we voiced our frustrations to our dad about how selfish we felt she was, he resolutely said:

"It's not her fault. We both decided this," reiterating what he had told us earlier.

I nodded my head but totally disagreed. In the back of my mind, I wondered if this was how Dad had interacted with Mom. Did he acquiesce without standing up for what he really believed? Did he suppress how he often felt, leading him to find someone with whom he could better connect?

Dad's health continued to deteriorate. The doctors let us know that his white blood cell count was continuing to be very high. A typical white blood cell count is in the 4,000 to 11,000 range. For those with leukemia, it can get as high as 100,000 to 400,000. I flew back to see Dad multiple times over the course of the next year. After we moved back to California, it was easier to either drive six hours or take a quick flight to see him in Phoenix.

During one trip to see him, he looked up at me in his hospital gown. His blanket was pulled up to his chest and his strong arms looked noticeably thinner. He turned his head toward me.

"Dave, can you get me a Bible?"

I hadn't talked to Dad about spiritual things ever since the Chevy incident. God and the church in the world used to be key parts of our everyday conversation, but now, even though I was leading a church, both of us felt uncomfortable talking about God or religious stuff.

"Sure, Dad. I'll get you a couple Bibles. There are some new translations that are much more understandable these days."

Dad smiled and nodded his head.

I couldn't believe Dad was asking for a Bible. It was remarkable, given the public shaming, disrespect, and hurt he'd experienced from the church where he'd been a popular volunteer leader. Overly enthusiastic about my dad's interest in God, I ordered him three translations that were more modern and readable than the King James. On my next visit, I was eager to hear how his Bible reading was doing. I asked, "How has the Bible reading been going? What do you think God is saying to you?"

He paused, then looked at me with a sincere expression of humility. Tears formed in his eyes. He said, "That I've been away too long."

That sounded like God to me. It wasn't condemning. It was gentle. God was saying He missed being with my father. God wasn't interested in dredging up Dad's past failures or mistakes but was just delighted that Dad wanted to be with Him again. Knowing my dad, he had beat himself up multiple times for the mistakes he'd made. He'd blurt out when he made a mistake, "Stupid!" "Idiot." Harsh words to curse yourself with. If this was what he said about himself audibly, I wondered how he spoke to himself internally.

My view of God was changing alongside my dad's. I no longer saw God as someone looking to shame you for your wrong choices. I now understood that God was someone who loved cheering you on, loving you, like my mom's best friend Kim Ahjumma did with Mom. Instead of God only desiring for us to believe in Him, He also wants us to know He believes in us. Instead of the God who is in heaven, ready to unleash punishment for all our wrongs, I was understanding God more like a loving father, ever present with us, whose love is like a waterfall. It never stops. In fact, if there is any one definition of God that is the most encompassing of who He is, it would be unconditional, ever-flowing, unstoppable love. While God's love was something addressed at our church growing up, fear was what I'd felt the most. It was more about being right than being loving. Judging each other's actions more than celebrating each other. The more I know of God, the more I see that love supersedes the rules and laws we tend to uphold.

Once again, I was seeing my dad more clearly. He became human. I asked God to give me His eyes for my father. And one day, something happened. I started to see my dad as a child. As Gary, the little boy who didn't have a father. He did the best he could with the resources and experiences he was given, which in many ways was better than I did. He was broken just like me. But also more beautiful than I gave him credit for.

❧

It was the year 2007, after I returned back to the States from Bangkok. Carolyn called me on the phone. Her voice trembled with fear. You could tell she was crying.

"Dave, your dad is not doing well," she said softly, her voice trembling. "They think he's going to pass anytime now. If you can come, you need to come right away."

"I'll be right there."

I flew back to Arizona and drove straight to the Mayo Clinic, not too far from where my dad lived in Phoenix. They lived near this beautiful mountain, and he would look at it every day, taking long drags on a cigarette. When I arrived, late in the afternoon, the Arizona sunset was magnificent. There is nothing like an Arizona sunset. God shows off His artistry with spectacular hues of purple, red, orange, and maroon. He paints the sky.

I went through the large lobby area and took an elevator to the floor where my dad was resting. Being a pastor, I've walked into many ICUs and hospital rooms. I usually try not to talk to the nurses as I make my way to a patient's room. The more confident and focused you are when you walk through the hospital, the more you're usually left alone. *Just act like you belong here,* I reminded myself. Finally, I found my dad's room. He was by himself. Carolyn was at home resting. By this time, her introverted and private self had had more than enough interaction. Doug had seen Dad earlier. I was sure my brother was having a difficult time processing not only the prospect of losing Dad but also Carolyn's role in persuading Dad to not continue the successful treatments in Houston. He's strong but, like my father, was probably internalizing most of his pain and emotions. Since I'm his brother, he wouldn't have to say anything. It's that mixture of jeong and han where words are not needed to express how you feel. You're connected by this collective love and pain. You just know.

In this large room with shiny floors, the digital equipment constantly monitoring his vitals, the only sounds were the occasional alarms and his rhythmic breathing. I placed my backpack down on the chair and settled myself next to the window, expecting to be there awhile. I gazed at my father. His once ripped, muscular frame was considerably weakened by all the chemo and medicines infused into his body over the past year.

The nurse walked in.

"Are you his son?"

"Yes. How is he doing?"

She quietly came next to me and whispered, "His organs are starting to fail. Water is filling his lungs. We have him on a morphine drip to ease any pain. It won't be long. I'll be outside if you need anything."

I just stared at Dad as he kept going in and out of consciousness.

He would occasionally reach his hand out, like he was trying to grab something in the air. I wondered if he was trying to touch an angel, or perhaps it was Mom that he was seeing as he was in this place between heaven and earth.

Dad woke up for a moment. Groggy, and with eyes half-shut, he looked at me. He had a serious look:

"Dave, will you make sure to take care of Carolyn?"

He had a sense of urgency in his voice. "Like we told you in the past, we want you to be our advocate and executor of anything we have. But, Dave, will you take care of Carolyn when I'm gone?"

I had an instinctive reaction to say something like, "You're not going to die." It's the positive, optimistic spirit that's become part of my pastoral response. But Dad knew he was about to pass. While I thought it, I couldn't bring myself to say anything empty or possibly untrue.

In the flash of a second, I thought how, a few years earlier, this request would have seemed utterly unfathomable. This was the woman who assisted in breaking up our family. She had devastated Mom, who was never the same again. But the anger and bitterness that I'd felt when Carolyn first came into our lives was gone. And the resentment I held about Carolyn's decision not to continue Dad's series of treatments in Houston was not there. Dad didn't have to agree with her; it was ultimately his choice.

He kept looking at me, waiting for my response. It's one thing to care for someone's estate, but to care for another person is another level of emotional buy-in. I would have severed my relationship with Carolyn after my dad's passing if it had been up to me. Dad knew that instinctively. He also knew the Bible well enough to know that the Christian ethic is about forgiveness and grace. He had me.

Seeing his earnestness, I couldn't say no.

"Of course, Dad," I told him.

But Dad wasn't convinced.

"Dave, you'll make sure she's taken care of? Promise me."

"Yes. I promise."

Hearing my promise, Dad exhaled and just closed his eyes.

You could feel his relief. He felt the responsibility to ask me, not Doug, not Carolyn's own son. I was the one that had the most trouble with her, and now I was going to be her primary caretaker. Odd. God has an odd sense of humor. But I guess God knew that I needed to be free of any weight from the past. This promise of acting on my dad's behalf in Carolyn's life was a way of reversing the curse they must have felt from us kids. I knew to find healing, I had to extend grace to the one who had wounded me. Forgiveness was more about my freedom from the past.

As evening came, Dad kept grasping for imaginary things in the air. I wondered if he was starting to see heavenly objects or people.

Just sitting there, looking at him in the cold confines of a sterile hospital room, my mind wandered. This is how life ends. In a cold barren hospital room, tied to machines monitoring your slow demise. People surround you, just sadly staring at you. Not everyone was here to say farewell. For my dad, it was just me. I felt sorry for him that I was the only one in the room. You'd expect a room to be filled with your partner, children, and grandchildren. Perhaps your own siblings and friends. But it was just me.

The sun had gone down and the cold night air started to settle slowly into the desert. Arizona can be hot during the day and cold at night. Memories of our times together flashed through my mind.

I heard him calling me "Nature Boy." I pictured all the times we cast our fishing lines with sharp barbed hooks near his face when we were learning how to fish, almost taking out one of his eyes. His startled expressions that would make my brother and me roll in laughter. I remembered his contagious guffaws and even his thunderous farts. He knew his farts would 100 percent always get a rise out of my brother and me. He was the champion fartmaster in our house, often showcasing his unique creative body movements to accentuate the vibrato. Then I also thought of my immaturity and how I'd treated him. The memories kept coming.

Thoughts of his childhood without a father, the good times with our family, the risks he took in moving his young family from Maryland to Arizona. I imagined the disappointment and the hurt he must have felt with his relationship with Mom. The pain of having children who later didn't respect him. Especially after all the years he'd been such a generous, humorous, and loving father. I felt the weight of the suffering he'd experienced. Where once he had enjoyed a good reputation and respect among his church friends, now all he faced was disdain or judgment because of his affair. They were gone. He had Carolyn but few friends.

Then one memory tucked away in the vault of my mind suddenly surfaced. It was right after I let him know how upset I was with him when he left Mom and us. He quickly, and somewhat cryptically, said, "You don't know everything."

What in the world had he meant by that? That was all he said. He didn't add any more information. No more color or definition. He left me hanging. I didn't want to ask for more because I had so little respect for him at the time. But I knew he was right. There are things between partners that only they know. That one statement only added to the mystery of Mom's past, her possible own failings in their divorce, and secrets I was never made aware of.

All this time, I'd never addressed these kinds of questions. It never felt necessary. Anything unspoken seemed like it needed to stay that way. We were not equipped to artfully unearth the past. My mom, culturally Korean, wouldn't want to bring it up because of our shame-based culture. And understanding Dad's impoverished past, raised by a single mom and brothers, I knew he didn't have the tools to talk about these types of hard things.

When confronting death, you see more clearly what is important and what is of less value. Marriage requires difficult conversations that most of us are ill equipped for, especially if you married young, like my parents did.

In every story, I spoke about my mom. She was always the protagonist. The hero.

Rarely in adulthood did I refer to my dad as a victim or as someone worthy of honor. Yet his approaching death unlocked something I didn't know was in me. My anger and resentment were a way of protecting myself from the pain of losing him. He was the father that all the kids had wanted to have. When our family was together, I could see in my friends' eyes that they wished they had a dad like mine. He was funny. Affectionate. Well read. A wordsmith. Lover of art and music. An entrepreneur who ran a successful business. Dad was physically fit and strong. Handsome and humble. He was extraordinary in the time he spent with us outdoors, camping, fishing, and then teaching us how to play baseball and football. For most of my life as a child, he was there for us. He was a part of that season in American history when the middle class grew larger, where many rose out of the generational poverty they experienced after World War II. He had sacrificed for us, like my mom did. He never defended himself or made excuses or blamed my mom for the failure of their marriage. The only thing he said was that last vague statement, that I didn't "know everything" about Mom or their relationship. He never spoke badly about Mom. He never admitted what he must have known to be true.

I thought about all the sacrifices he'd made, not sharing his secrets or deep pain with us. At the time, I still wondered what Mom had done or said that might have been so hurtful to him. But given a lifetime of opportunity to defend himself and to shift the blame to Mom, he never did, and I respected my father for that.

As I sat there in that hospital room, night had come. The room was dimly lit so Dad could sleep. Dad suddenly woke up.

"Dave, can you help me turn over?"

"Sure, Dad."

I stood up. He lifted his arm up to hold on to mine. Then he gripped on to my arm. He pulled himself up to reposition his body so he could face me, lying on his right side.

I sat down and we locked eyes. He then slowly closed his. Took a few more breaths. I heard one last exhale. And the stillness came.

The nurse had already turned down the volume of the heartbeat monitor so there wouldn't be any noise. But I looked up and saw he had flatlined. Unsure, I stepped outside. I looked for a nurse. It seemed so anticlimactic. No one outside that room had any comprehension that my dad had just died. I saw a nurse at the nursing station.

"Uhhh, ma'am, I think my father just passed away."

The nurse walked back with me to the room and examined him. Looked at all the monitors and started turning them off.

"Yes, your dad is no longer here. I'm sorry. We'll call the funeral home. And we can take it from here. They'll take care of him. You can stay longer if you want, but it's okay for you to go home."

Just like that, on February 13, 2007, my dad died. And with him went secrets I never will know.

But there was one thing I did know in that room where it was just me and him. We had worked through the hurt. We saw each other. We had forgiven each other. We had forgiven ourselves.

I kissed my father one last time.

CHAPTER TWENTY-TWO

Same Same

Y ou're the man of the house now."
My mom's words echoed in my heart for a long time after my dad's passing. I had refused to accept these words when she'd said them to me after their divorce. But when my dad died, I felt like I really was the "man of the house" now. Yet I still felt like a boy in many ways. And I certainly didn't feel adequate. A lot of life isn't about choice; you're just thrust into it, responding to what you need to do.

For years, I struggled with owning my role as father. I'd feel that lack and disconnect constantly, all through my own children's earliest years. Yet all the time, even daily, I would be reminded of how I was a father figure, not just to our children, but to many others I was serving. People would come up to me after I spoke or when they read something I wrote:

"You're like a father to me."

"You remind me of my dad."

"I want to be a part of your family."

"You are like the dad I never had."

Even if they didn't say it out loud, I could still see it in their eyes. They looked at me and saw someone who they thought could love them in a way their own father didn't. That was consistently frightening for me.

When it came to my pastoral work, I was constantly placed in a fatherly role, whether I liked it or not. As early as when I was in my twenties in ministry, I could see people looking at me like I was their father.

Our Newsong church community's demographic was really young, so I carried the weight of being a father for the many who I knew had difficult relationships with their dads. While it may seem like a compliment for someone to say that I'm like a father to them, I found myself conflicted. First of all, it was hard to see myself as a mature man. I still felt like a boy. Being seen as a father to so many made me feel old. And second of all, I didn't want to disappoint them, their expectations. I had already experienced individuals projecting their dad issues onto me, and I had enough drama personally interacting with my own father while still trying to be a good father to my own children.

Hearing comments like this always made me feel uncomfortable. Outwardly, I'd smile, but inwardly, I'd say to myself, *Man, I'm not your dad! I don't want to be your dad. And I don't think you want me to be your dad. I'm sure I'll disappoint you.*

When it came to my own four children, two seemingly contradictory truths were becoming clearer in my life. The first was that I felt like I was the luckiest man on the planet because I was the father of four beautiful, creative, and spiritual children. Their relationships with one another were intimate, fun, and secure. The second truth was that, even though I loved them, being their father unearthed a deep sense of inadequacy within me. There was this constant feeling that I would never be enough for them. It felt like there was some invisible force that was keeping me from engaging them more deeply. Hence, I brought many good uncle- and aunt-like people into my kids' lives because, one, if I were to die prematurely, they would have these other parental figures to lean on, and two, I felt that if their maturity depended on me alone, it was going to be woefully inadequate. They would need a village to help raise them to be their best selves.

For years, I just kept going, ignoring my doubts and conflicted feelings about being a father. I really didn't know where they were coming from. Until a young leader came into my life named Nick Roach.

In 2012, the chaplain for the Chicago Bears, a new friend, asked me if I would give a message to the team. Was he kidding? I love football. My dream in high school had been to be the first Korean American NFL professional football player. I jumped on a plane from Orange County to San Francisco. I had been invited to speak in the pre-game chapel service for the Chicago Bears. These chapels were held several hours before the game since most couldn't attend their home places of worship because they had to work on weekends. While I didn't fulfill my childhood dream of playing in the NFL, this was the next best thing. Empowering these young leaders to grow personally, relationally, and spiritually was right in my sweet spot even if it was just one talk.

As the large men and their coaches came filing into the room in their warm-ups, shorts, and T-shirts, I couldn't believe I was in this situation. I was trying to hold back my excitement. I recognized several of the players who were All-Pros that you'd see eating someone's lunch on the field.

The Bears chaplain was introduced and I shared some inspiring thoughts. Afterward, one by one, these behemoths of humanity came up to me and shook my hand. Some gave me a hug. I was laughing because, when they embraced me, I felt like a child being squeezed by a grizzly bear. My head would land around their stomach or chest area. Others came up to me and said, "Hey, man, don't tell the coaches this, but pray for me. I have some injuries that need healing." I discovered that players tend not to discuss chronic or even severe injuries because they fear they are more vulnerable to being taken out of play and being relegated to the bench. Many of these players would suffer concussions during practices or games, which could lead to more severe mental health challenges, brain atrophy, and death. Listening to them, I realized they are the modern gladiators sacrificing their bodies for the bloodthirsty crowd. America loves violence. The force of helmet-to-helmet hits is similar to the intensity of being in a collision with another car.

As the line was nearing the end, this young, gentle-looking guy came up to me. He didn't look like a linebacker. He felt like someone who could just as easily have been an artist or a professor instead of a football player. He said, "I'm Nick Roach..." Suddenly his head went into my shoulder and he just started weeping. He was blubbering. Losing it. This was not what a starting middle linebacker does before his most important game of the season in front of a national audience! But I knew these were the type of tears that came from a deep place. He kept sobbing.

In this very vulnerable moment, Nick shed tears that had been bottled up inside him for years.

"Can you stay around after everybody else leaves so we can talk?" I suggested to Nick.

Before the two of us sat down together, I asked God what I should say to him. Soon we were on our own, a few players lingering around to further a conversation with me but patiently waiting for me to finish up with Nick.

I looked at Nick as he was still wiping tears from his eyes.

"I could be wrong, but I think God wants you to know He has you where you are for a reason," I said. "Nick, believe it and stop doubting. I see a picture of a mouth, and it feels like God wants you to open your mouth. There's a lot in your mind. You like to stay quiet, but from now on, when people ask you for your input, you need to speak up. You have an important voice. There will come a time when people want to and will need to hear what you have to say. In fact, people may be surprised because you're a football player but you are also a creative. An artist. A communicator."

Nick was shocked by how accurate these words were. These were the very things he had been contemplating at that moment in his life. He was one of the best athletes in the world, but football really didn't matter to him. He was ready to give it up. He could easily have another successful career with the many creative gifts he possessed.

"Dave, everything, I mean everything, you're saying about me is spot on. That's crazy."

"Nick, I'll be in Chicago in a couple weeks. Let's connect then. I'd love to meet your wife too. What's her name?"

"Anna-Marie."

"Yes, I'll meet her, as well, and we can do a formal consult. We can meet at my hotel."

"That would be great. Thanks, Dave."

We exchanged numbers. I walked away from that day feeling like it was one of the best days of my life. I got to feel like I was part of the team but didn't have to get my body beat up or my brain potentially damaged from the constant hitting and tackling. That moment was memorable because of Nick's vulnerability and how we seemed to have connected. It was love at first sight. He felt like a family member to me. Like a son.

Nick and Anna-Marie came to see me in Chicago. They treated me like family from day one. But it didn't feel as odd for some reason as it normally did. The ease of our relationship was unusual, and the trust organic. They began calling me "Father Dave" or "Papa Dave." Nick told me he wanted to be mentored by me and travel with me around the world to learn everything I know about developing people and leaders. Impacted by our interaction, he believed the adviser/consultant type of work I do could also be something he could do post-NFL.

Since that *Monday Night Football* day many years ago, Nick and Anna-Marie have had six beautiful children! And I don't think they're stopping! These little ones now also call me "Papa Dave" or "Father Dave." When Nick and Anna-Marie's children see me, they run to me and jump into my arms like I'm their grandpops. They are genuinely happy to see me. "Papa Dave, tell us another story! Please. Do you have anything to eat?" I knew the only way the kids could be this comfortable with me was because Nick and Anna-Marie spoke fondly about me to their children. I was familiar to them because of how often I was discussed. I'm family.

But despite all these feel good things, why did I still feel awkward being called "Papa Dave"?

One day, I asked Nick why he called me "Papa Dave" like it was the most natural thing in the world. He told me he started calling me this when he was processing his own fatherhood. As he was thinking about how he wanted to equip his kids and bring them up, Nick said he found himself drawing on a lot of what he had learned from me. He said that not only had I given him information on how to be a good dad, but I'd modeled it directly for him.

"I realized you'd played a greater, more impactful father role than anyone else in my life, and that I would never have had the type of love and unity we have in my family without you."

I couldn't believe he was talking about me. I felt like I was a horrible dad. Others seemed so much better than me. I said to myself, *Nick must have such a low threshold to compare me with.* For all Nick's sincere sharing, I still found myself struggling with the idea that I was Papa Dave, and that I could be a good father. It didn't feel that way with even my own children. My own children never said I was not a good father, but I've seen great dads like Nick, and I pale in comparison. Nick eventually left the NFL because of the multiple concussions he sustained while playing, and now he relishes the opportunity to be a "house dad." Nick gladly accepted the full-time job of loving, teaching, and guiding his children, along with Anna-Marie. These kids are brilliant and are being taught Spanish and English and probably Mandarin next.

Nick was becoming more like a son to me every time I saw him.

It was the way he looked at me, the way he hugged me, the way he talked about me, the way he encouraged me, the way he wanted to listen to me, the way he thought about me, the way he wanted to be with me. He knows I have faults but he chose to focus on what is good about who I am. But something, too, was unexplainable in our connection.

Seeing myself through Nick's eyes started changing me. I realized that my complicated relationship with my father—who had an absent father—was affecting my relationship with my children. To have Nick Roach, a son who didn't have a strong relationship with his father, now have a relationship with me unlocked what was suppressed in me.

What was this unexplainable connection? It must be that Korean jeong thing.

One day Nick and I were casually talking when the day he was born was brought up.

"Hey, Nick, when is your birthday?"

"I was born June 16, 1985."

My mouth dropped.

This was the very same day and year Rebecca had a miscarriage and we lost our first child, whom we rarely spoke about.

The very same day.

CHAPTER TWENTY-THREE

This Is Me

I was doing a fair amount of speaking around this time, traveling around the world to give a talk to a group of entrepreneurs in Bangkok or to a group of NFL athletes ready to play on *Monday Night Football*, or to Silicon Valley technologists, or to Wall Street's fund managers. Everywhere I went, from California to New York to Bangkok to São Paulo to Seoul to Singapore, I started my talk the same way. It went something like this:

"Hi, I'm Dave Gibbons."

I always paused after saying my name.

"I know it's hard to believe. You were probably expecting a white guy with the name 'Gibbons.' Well, believe it or not, I'm half-Korean and half-white. My mom is a beautiful five-feet-tall Korean woman with tons of passion, the kind that doesn't care what people think. And my dad is a white guy from Michigan with blue eyes."

Once again I would pause, letting the anticipation and curiosity grow.

Then with perfect comedic timing, I would say:

"Looking at me, you can tell Koreans have some strong genes!"

Audiences always laughed at that. People loved that line. And it answered the pressing question most people had when they saw me for the first time: "How does a hundred percent Asian-looking guy get a name like Gibbons?" (Probably the second-most pressing question was, "How come he speaks English with no accent?")

While everyone was laughing, there was always one person who never cracked a smile if she happened to be in the audience: Rebecca. Her face would let you know what she thought. After being in a Korean church, she started to question whether I was half-white and half-Korean. Later she would come to the conclusion that I was 100 percent Korean. She had never met a Korean before me, which I thought was proof she didn't know what she was talking about.

When I finally decided to talk to her about it after we had been married for a while, I came ready to plead my case like a lawyer.

"When I was young, I went to my dad and asked who I was. 'Am I Korean or American?' And he got defensive, almost angry. He told me 'Of course you're American.' Dad wouldn't lie to me. He said to me with conviction that I was American, meaning white."

I proceeded to make my second point.

"When I got older, there were moments I wondered. My half sister was fully Korean; Dad had adopted her when he married Mom. What if I was adopted, too? Then I realized all I had to do was look at my birth certificate."

I handed Becca my birth certificate so she could see it. It said my father was Gary W. Gibbons and my mom was Son Chae Hong.

Then lastly, I let Becca know that, "I've talked to friends who are scientists and geneticists. I asked, 'Is it possible that I can be a child of a white man and a Korean mom and look a hundred percent Korean?' They said 'Absolutely.'"

Becca listened and nodded and said she understood. But whenever the subject came up, she would remain silent, her body language communicating that she wasn't buying it. My wife is a woman of complete honesty. Her face will not lie about what she's feeling. Truth and complete honesty, no matter how painful, is what Becca is all about.

After my father had passed away, I felt it was time to get to the bottom of the question. The truth of my roots. I wanted to settle this once and for all. I was looking forward to Becca discovering she was absolutely wrong.

Without telling Becca, I ordered a DNA test, a kit where you take a cotton swab of your saliva in your mouth and send it back to be processed. With each step, I was already celebrating her imminent capitulation. I relished each moment that brought me closer to being proved right. I couldn't wait to say, "I told you so." But I planned not to say a word after handing her the test results. I would just smile and let her feel the energy of my delightful gloating.

The day I received the e-mail with my results, I quickly clicked the link to go online to see my ancestral roots. I was already getting giddy about the results, which I was preparing to print and show to Rebecca. There it was, a color wheel displaying the breakdown of my ethnic roots, showing that I am genetically...

100 percent Asian.

What?!!

At that time, the results showed that I was around 80 percent Korean, 10 percent Japanese, and there were also some Chinese origins and a little Southeast Asian. But as the years passed and more people took the genetic test, the accuracy of the data got better. My results now convincingly confirm that I'm 100 percent Korean.

Like a dog with its tail curled, slowly walking to the master, I reluctantly approached my wife.

"Rebecca, I took a genetic test. Guess what? I'm not Caucasian at all. I'm 100 percent Asian, most likely pure Korean."

Becca smiled. She didn't gloat or rub it in, but I knew she was pretty dang happy. She was all smiles inside her. She had known it all along. My four kids were surprised, and then concerned for me, worried about how I would take the news. I had essentially lived with this false understanding of my bi-ethnic racial identity my entire life.

Oddly enough, I wasn't rocked by this revelation, because I'd lived with the remote possibility of this conclusion for years. But I would counter any question of my ethnic origins with what my dad told me when he said I was "American." Truth is, he didn't actually say I was from European roots, that I was "white." He didn't say I was his biological son. Technically, he could still be honest by saying that I was culturally and legally an American, an American citizen.

Or, I wondered, what if he didn't know that I had a different birth father? Had he guessed, but never known for sure? Was this what he had meant when he'd told me I didn't "know everything" about Mom? I wondered if he discovered that he wasn't my birth father. That must have been shocking for him. Could I have been the reason he started distancing himself from Mom, and then eventually having his affair with Carolyn?

I'll never know.

Who was my biological father? What did he look like? What were his traumas? Was he responsible? Did he take advantage of my mother? I have searched with private detectives and government agencies, and have even gone to Korea to find him, but with no success. I'm still searching for my biological father. Still wondering if he's alive. How am I like him?

"Chong, you're not going to believe this," I said to my sister. "I took a DNA test hoping to show Rebecca that I'm genetically American as well as Korean. However, the test results came back and revealed that I'm a hundred percent Korean. Did you know?"

"Dave, I didn't know. I always thought you were like Doug, a blend of Mom and Dad."

"Well, that's not what the test says." Then, I had a startling thought. "I wonder if your birth father is my birth father?"

"I don't know," Chong said with a stunned look.

This sent me on a quest to unveil this enigma of my birth father. I started with a search for my only living relative I knew on my mother's side, Uncle Sung Hwan, who had resided with us in Arizona while he adapted to life in America. But his whereabouts were mysterious; he was possibly somewhere in Texas and rumored to be divorced. At the time, my search for him proved fruitless. Then I went to Mom's best friend, Kim Ahjumma. She now had dementia and didn't know. Yet I wondered if she was holding things back because of a possible promise she made to Mom.

Eventually, I'd travel to Korea, enlisting the service of a well-connected detective procured by a friend. I went to the city my mom called home to uncover the truth. I was told police stations keep meticulous records of residents. Serendipitously, a friend's father—a humble and prominent figure in a local megachurch in the same city where my mother lived—had connections throughout the city. These connections included the chief of police and a leader of a radio station and a news outlet. Becca and I conscientiously engaged with each person hoping they might point us to the key to unlock the information about my birth father. I engaged in interviews trying to get national attention to my plight both in print and social media. But no new information emerged. The identity of my birth father would still be a mystery.

Accompanying me was a younger friend who was adopted. He, too, was traveling to Korea with us to pursue knowledge of his biological roots. He had difficulty as well, yet he was able to procure his birth certificate, revealing the stigmatizing phrase "illegitimate child" on one of the lines.

Although my birth certificate bore no such derogatory label, I couldn't ignore the stark reality that I would have been branded as such if circumstances hadn't aligned to connect me to my American father.

❧

My DNA results initially triggered a profound sense of astonishment—an undeniable revelation that upended my perception of self. However, as I gradually processed this truth, the fact that I was 100 percent Korean didn't trouble me. Curiously, a therapist connected to my family speculated that this newly uncovered secret might cause a traumatic episode for me, discovering that my biological father wasn't the one I had always assumed. The passage of time and the wisdom of years, however, allowed me to embrace this reality with understanding. Despite the enigma of my birth father's identity, I am fortunate to have had a father who steadfastly loved me the best he could. And while my dad didn't fulfill every expectation, individuals like Nick or Dave Bunt stepped in to bridge those gaps. Numerous people have assumed the roles of nurturing figures—both fatherly and motherly. Among them, Nick, for instance, saw facets of me that were obscured from my own view.

So I am a wonderful, spicy, salty, and sweet fusion of cultures, 100 percent Korean and 100 percent American.

CHAPTER TWENTY-FOUR

Epiphany

R ebecca was softly crying, barely audible. Her body turned away from mine. For a moment I hesitated to say anything.

I hustled between the two worlds of business and institutionalized religion. I was still struggling with the operational side of leading a faith community that was integrating and collaborating with the city and county leaders. Our church was in the middle of the transition from the upper-middle-class educational environment of Irvine, California, to Santa Ana's more urban, Latin, Hispanic, Mexican culture. I had gone through the difficult process of downsizing a large staff who focused on program to a team centered more around people and their dreams. Transitioning staff is not easy; it feels personal. Some of the people I had to let go were friends and longtime associates. The young leaders saw me more like a father than a senior leader, so it was especially painful. I often felt misunderstood, hurt, and betrayed. Worse, I now recognized that I made other people feel the same way, too. The feelings of betrayal are the most difficult for me to personally overcome. If something smells of betrayal, my body goes back to that day my mom locked herself up in that car.

I used to say that it's harder to be a leader in a for-profit space than a nonprofit. Having worked in both spheres now, I have changed my mind on this and believe being a leader in a nonprofit space is much more challenging. You have to take care of all the same types of systems, but also raise capital from donations and work with primarily a volunteer crew. But at this time of my life, most of my work was like I was driving an all-terrain vehicle, but it seemed my new calling was to start doing the dirty, detailed work under the hood of the car. I felt my life was focused on the very thing that was not my strength and gave me the least energy. I felt like I was physically aging, filled with constant anxiety about people. Their criticisms, their expectations, and their needs were a part of who I was. It was my job to help others share their burdens with me and our team.

While I was in this crisis mode, I really didn't want to go into a protracted conversation with Becca that night. I was tired.

Maybe Becca just needs this alone time without me intruding on her.

As much as I tried to reason with myself, this didn't feel right. So finally, as tenderly as I could, I asked, *"Becca, why are you crying?"*

"I felt God spoke to me." She paused. "I know you need your sleep, and it can wait till morning."

Becca doesn't ever speak this way. In fact, she thinks people should be more careful making such pronouncements like, "God told me to tell you this." She's seen how some have claimed it was God but it obviously wasn't. That's why her saying this was quite unusual.

At that time, the church was facing severe headwinds. People were struggling with my leadership, vision, direction, decisions on staff, and our financial picture. It was probably the lowest point in the life of our church. It felt like we were going through the slow death of a dream. Yet what was happening was that all the important elements of the dream were being reimagined into something that was going to help the church flourish for generations to come. We were doing the ugly, behind-the-scenes dirty work of reorganizing the church to adapt to who the world was becoming.

I knew I was not in a good state of health or mind. I found myself tired. Irritable. Easily upset. And pointing fingers at people who I felt had betrayed or abandoned me at church. Also, I was bitter with Becca because she, too, had shared with me that I shouldn't leave Newsong even though I was suffering. I thought she cared more about what I'd helped to build than she cared about me. It had gotten to the point that a few years before this, before coming back from my time in Bangkok, I had asked my best friends and Becca to please understand that I was not supposed to be the one to lead the church to its next season. I felt it would kill the church and destroy me in the process if I had to carry the church. The responsibility of starting the church weighed heavily on me. I couldn't just leave when things were dramatically changing in our world. So until I could at least get Newsong back on track for the next person to take over, I was committed to seeing the church through, just putting my head down each day and trying to hustle harder to keep the community from falling apart. When things go well, everyone seems like your friend. When the sheesh hits the fan, you feel alone, even though that is not entirely true.

As I was dealing with my own personal challenges, a rising chorus of people at church were letting their sentiments be known. Mainly because they felt abandoned when I left for Thailand for a year. I realized that my challenges were overlooked when our church was buzzing with success, but they became glaringly evident when our community started struggling.

Becca had been getting strong impressions she felt from God for about a year. Each time, she'd been alarmed by what she was feeling. The third time, she had an impression of words that were so lucid, she immediately ran and got a pen and paper to write them down. Again, all this is not normal for Becca because she's witnessed the spiritual abuse of leaders claiming their ideas were from God.

With fear and trepidation, I said to her, "You can tell me now. What did God say to you?"

"You are so concerned about monetary debt, yet the debt of offense you have against others is far greater. Only when you take care of your own debt of offense will you not only be a leader, but also become a leader of leaders."

Nahhhhh. This isn't from God. God wouldn't say that knowing what I've been through. If anyone needs to apologize, it's them.

God knew the people Becca was referring to, the same ones who had talked trash behind my back and betrayed me while I couldn't say or do anything. I began thinking of what it would look like to go to them and ask for forgiveness where I'd offended them. Becca fell asleep, but I couldn't do the same. My frustration continued to build as I thought about all the people who I believed had hurt me or my family. I went through people who had spoken disparagingly about me. People whom I know longer saw. People I really didn't want to think about anymore. They had become hostile toward me. Some had even deeply wounded me.

But how have I wounded them?

Until this moment, I hadn't thought too deeply about this. I was ready to dismiss this as certainly not being from God. Yet this phrase "leader of leaders" struck me.

I had heard people say this about me for a long time. Early mentors in high school, like Pastor Dave Bunt, had said that I would become a leader of leaders. My mentors from graduate school and leadership initiatives, and finally another leader I grew to respect, from the San Francisco area, had said that exact phrase to me a few years prior over a breakfast in San Jose. The phrase had become embedded in my purpose, and it's one that has resonated with me through my whole life, even in seasons I've tried to run from it.

I wasn't able to sleep that night. By five in the morning, I found myself staring at the wall in the dark and admitting the truth.

That was God speaking to Becca.

So I got up and started making a list of the people whom I could possibly have hurt or offended.

It was a long list.

One by one I made my way through that list of names over the next several months.

From former staff to people I now really wanted nothing to do with.

It was definitely painful but with each person there was a gift of freedom awaiting me and the person I might have offended.

I was surprised how in the middle of conversations I would start to see the person who I felt was talking smack behind my back or sending bad energy my way looking like a child. Not in a negative way, but in a way where they looked innocent, hurt, and just wanting to be loved.

He was the first person on my list that I called. His offense seemed obvious to me. At a time when the organization I was overseeing was struggling financially, he'd had the audacity to ask for a raise. And on top of that to say he worked "just as hard" as I did. I felt like I was listening to a teenage rant. But there I was sitting at the table, listening to him, years after not talking to him, and magically, I couldn't believe this emotion rising up in me. He suddenly felt like a son to me. The realization tore through my defensiveness and judgmental arrogance. Beyond the demands and the attitude that were hard for me to get over in the past, I now saw his pain, his disappointment and suffering at my inability even to understand or empathize with his life.

My past responses were so defensive that it had been hard for me to hear him or feel his pain.

My wife's tears had brought me to this epiphany but something also changed in the way I saw him. It was love. The feelings that one has for their own child started overwhelming me.

After having gone to most of the people on that list, I made a discovery: a person's identity may rest in what they think they're not. If we get rocked in an area that is considered our strength, we can easily become demoralized. Sometimes our greatest calling resides in the place of our deepest wounds. There were reasons I struggled with the idea of fatherhood. It primarily had to do with my own father. Then suddenly I was walloped by the truth that the reason I was running away from being a father was that I was scared to hurt my children like my dad hurt us. I didn't want to disappoint my children. So why even try to be a father? I discovered the answer over time that being a father is my inheritance. Both my mom and dad struggled without fathers. My sister didn't know her father. And I don't know my birth father. But my guess is that although all of the fathers in our family's histories made mistakes, they were good fathers. Within me is the power to be a good father.

CHAPTER TWENTY-FIVE

The Promise Fulfilled

D ave. Can you hold … my hand?"

I haven't heard Carolyn speak this way before. There is an urgency in her voice. I look at her closely; she's struggling. She looks frightened. Her eyes are enlarged.

I realize she is having a panic attack.

I quickly grab her hand and try to soothe her.

"Carolyn, try to breathe more slowly. I'll call the nurse but I think she's with somebody right now. I hear her in another room."

"Dave, it's still hard for me to breathe."

Earlier in the day I sat down with Carolyn and the nurse and physician. They had just expressed to me their concern for her declining appetite—one of the signs that the end is near.

In just three short years, Carolyn has gone from an energetic senior to someone who suffers from dementia and has trouble walking. We'd had to transfer her out of the beautiful senior living center, where she had her own private condo. Originally she had thought it was too expensive, but we encouraged her to go for it. She deserved it. All of her life she had been extra careful about spending money. Carolyn was a saver and had learned to be frugal, having been divorced and a single mother before she met my father. After being in the senior living center for a few months and loving it, Carolyn fell and struck her head. After the doctors examined her, they said she would need a more dedicated facility to assist her. She couldn't be alone. We had to move her out of her dream retirement condominium complex.

She did not like the idea of an assisted living facility. She was private, and liked to keep to herself. But it was the best thing for her since she didn't want to live in California with me and Becca. She loved Arizona. But more important for her, she didn't want to be a burden on us.

As I look at her face now, once again bruised from a more recent fall, Carolyn looks into my eyes to see any hint of what I may be thinking about her condition. She can smell any BS, so I've learned not to act like she looks good when she doesn't. She'll call me out on it. In the early days of her dementia, she would ask me how she was doing. I would say, "You're doing pretty good, Carolyn. In fact, I think you're doing fine, maybe even better than before."

"Yeah, right, Dave," she'd say. "I'm not better than I was before. I keep forgetting things."

She looks closely at me again to see if I'm concerned about her shortness of breath. I am, but I am trying not to show it. As she tries to read my thoughts, I see her struggling with her breathing. Gasping for air. I say to her, "Carolyn, what if I carry you to the room?" I can say this because she now weighs about 80 pounds.

"No, it's okay."

"Okay, I'll help you get up and we'll walk very slowly to your bed."

I help her stand. She holds on to one of my arms. I make sure to put my other arm around her waist to support her. We take small, measured steps to the room. As I am closely by her side, I notice how frail she is. As we get to her bed, I help her sit on the side of it. I then lift her legs. Place her under the covers and help situate her pillow. Finally, she closes her eyes to calm herself down.

Her breathing starts to come back to normal. And she falls asleep.

I make my way back to the living room and sit down.

The nurse comes over shortly and says, "Mr. Gibbons, I just checked on Carolyn. Her oxygen levels are good."

"Is she still sleeping?"

"Yes."

"Great!"

The nurse looks at me and smiles. I feel relieved I was here to help her walk through that moment. While Carolyn has dementia, her mind is still very sharp as you speak to her. Her long-term memory isn't good but her ability to be witty and observant is still keen. She knows that she is slowly dying. But the nurses say she forgets whether she's eaten. She's getting weaker and weaker as evidenced by her repeated falls.

It still surprises me every time I visit Carolyn that I'm actually talking to her.

During an earlier visit, I was sitting near her in the kitchen, and she wanted to make sure I knew the people sitting around her. If she didn't introduce me, people would introduce themselves or just stare at her. A ninety-plus-year-old former lawyer who had trouble speaking was being visited by her late-sixties daughter, a retired pediatrician. The daughter turned to her mother and they both said hi to me. The retired pediatrician turned back to her mom. "Isn't he good-looking?" I heard her whisper to her mom, but loud enough for me to hear. "He's nice eye candy." Her mom just smiled, as she has difficulty speaking, and looked at me. I tried to act like I hadn't heard her daughter's "whisper." I'd never been called "eye candy" before. I found it humorous, especially coming from another senior citizen in this nursing home.

Carolyn was sitting back watching it all. You'd find her often quietly amused by the people around this dinner table. When they all sat at the table for a meal, the stories and the comments were hilarious. It could be a reality show, for fellow seniors only, of course.

While at first Carolyn didn't like the idea of living in a large residential home with others, she has grown to love it. She never wants to leave.

Despite having dementia, and no matter how much she has forgotten over the years, she didn't forget my name. When I visited her for the first time, she proudly introduced me to the room of residents all in a row of La-Z-Boy chairs watching television or sleeping in their recliners: "Hey, everyone, this is my son." But this last time when I stopped by, she just gazed at me and smiled. "You look familiar." I said, "Yes, I'm your son, David."

It took me a moment as I was startled by her decline. The nurses had told me this day was coming.

I'm standing next to Carolyn's bed now.

She's still sleeping. I'm wondering how much more time I have left with her. My mind wanders to that last moment before my dad took his final breath and he asked me:

"Dave, will you make sure to take care of Carolyn?"

As I stand there looking at her, thinking about our relationship over the years, I am grateful for her. And thankful that this has come full circle.

I don't want to wake her. So I slowly make my way out of her bedroom. Go up to the nurses and let them know I'll be back soon. But I have to go back to California.

"Since she's declining quickly, I'll try to come more frequently.

And by the way, I left one of Carolyn's favorite desserts on the counter in the kitchen. You know the Korean cake, which isn't as sweet as the typical American cakes that Carolyn loves. It has strawberries and blueberries on it."

"Mr. Gibbons, we'll make sure Carolyn gets a slice."

"Great, but it's for everybody here. See you soon. Thank you so much for taking good care of Carolyn."

I head to my rental car, parked outside Carolyn's senior care home. As I open the door to leave the house, the Arizona heat torches my face. The temperature rising from the asphalt streets is about 20 degrees hotter than under the shade of a tree.

I get inside the car. Turn on the air-conditioning.

I buckle my seat belt and start to make my way to Sky Harbor Airport in Phoenix. As I drive away from the house, I can't help but smile and whisper: "Dad, I kept my promise."

Epilogue

My wife and I embarked on an immersive journey through Korea. This trip was a whirlwind historic tour of my ancestral homeland alongside some friends. Our itinerary was full of visits to museums as we traversed the beautiful landscapes on a chartered bus. In the middle of our trip, we anticipated spending a night in a historic village that mirrored the lifestyle of my ancestors. The quaint locale bore the name "Jeonju Hanok Village"—a collection of over eight hundred traditional Korean houses known as hanoks.

As we ventured through this charming enclave, the eye-catching stuccoed facades adorned with distinctly Asian rooftops captured our attention. Stepping inside, we found wooden floors that radiated warmth throughout the house—a heartening comfort during cold winter nights. There were no conventional Western beds; instead, we encountered neatly rolled-out blankets strewn across the floor. Sleeping atop traditional Korean bedding, cocooned beneath a cozy quilt, provided an authentic historic experience.

Being a light sleeper, I have developed particular preferences over the years. The pillow must be of the downy variety. The bed and room cool to the skin, a sanctum of tranquility. At home in the States, my comfortable California king mattress is a necessary part of my experience. Consequently, when I laid my eyes on what appeared to simply be a somewhat thick blanket accompanied by a small pillow, I worried that a restless sleep on these hard floors was ahead for me. I was already feeling a touch of self-pity. A first world problem for sure.

Nevertheless, I laid aside these concerns and hoped for the best, however elusive that might be on this cold winter night.

To my astonishment, I didn't wake up till morning even once.

Usually, I'll wake up at least once a night and get up very early. But I was out! I was completely enveloped by a deep and restful sleep.

My wife, who slept very badly that night, later confided that I was so serenely still and quiet all night, and even past the usual wake-up time, that she thought I might have died. She recounted how she leaned in, cautiously placing her finger close to my nose just to confirm that I was breathing!

"Dave, you slept so well. You never made a sound or moved all night long. I was scared. I didn't know if you were still alive."

I mused, "Hmmm, I don't know why I slept so well."

It was only later, when I looked at my birth certificate, that a profound realization washed over me. The very place where I had nestled into a deep slumber and an unprecedented stillness was none other than my mother's hometown.

In that moment, I knew I was home.

Acknowledgments

Chong and Doug, the journey wasn't easy, but we did all right. Mom and Dad would be proud of you both.

A heartfelt thank you to Inez, Travis, editors, proofreaders, and endorsers for generously contributing your expertise, encouragement, insights, and guidance throughout the creation of this memoir.

To all my friends featured in these pages and the institutions referenced, your influence and support have deeply shaped my life, and for that, I am profoundly grateful.

ABOUT THE AUTHOR

Dave Gibbons intrepidly explores the world, blending into crowded street markets, diverse cultures, and vibrant communities. He delights in leisurely strolls through unfamiliar cities, indulging in unique pastries, and immersing himself in the inventive designs of local creatives.

If Dave were to savor one final meal on earth, he would undoubtedly choose Korean barbecue, featuring thinly sliced beef and accompanied by Bibinaemyun (spicy Korean buckwheat noodles).

While Dave embraces all music genres, he particularly finds solace in the soothing melodies of classical compositions and simple instrumentals that allow the mind to wander and find repose.

Dave cherishes solitude, relishing private moments with friends and family. For him, home transcends physical location, residing wherever meaningful relationships flourish.

Dave seems to defy the aging process, maintaining a youthful vigor as the years pass. Firm in his belief that "Asians don't raisin," he exudes a radiant glow, especially after applying a rejuvenating Korean face mask.

To stay connected with Dave, follow him on his Instagram: @davekgibbons; or his X account: @davegibbons; and be sure to visit his website at DAVEGIBBONS.ORG.